BY BUS
TO SCHOOL

First published 2009

ISBN 978 0 7110 3403 7

Published by Ian Allan Publishing

an imprint of Ian Allan Publishing Ltd, Hersham, Surrey, KT12 4RG
Printed in England by Ian Allan Printing Ltd, Hersham, Surrey, KT12 4RG

Code: 0909/B

Visit the Ian Allan Publishing website at www.ianallanpublishing.com

BY BUS TO SCHOOL

Compiled by
GAVIN BOOTH

Contents

Introduction

The idea for this book followed the realisation that many of the best-known bus company managers, transport journalists and enthusiasts can date their interest in buses back to their schooldays. In the days before the school gates became clogged up with doting parents in 4x4s dropping off and collecting their little darlings, a bus was the obvious way to get to school and back again. And not a special school bus either, as schoolchildren crowded on with everybody else heading for their workplace. The sights, sounds and smells of these buses made such an impression on many of the contributors to this book that they decided to apply for jobs with bus companies when they left school or university.

The young Gavin Booth poses in 1951, age eight, proudly showing off his school prize. He wears 'whites' – the all-white version of the Royal High School uniform that was fortunately reserved for special occasions.

For others it was the realisation that all buses were not the same, that there were different companies running these buses, that the buses had unique registration and fleet numbers, that inspired an interest in buses that may never have led them to a career in transport, but drew them to a lifelong interest. These are the people whose interest matured and are the historians, writers and photographers whose knowledge fills the pages of countless books and magazines.

When I approached a range of 'bus people' asking them to contribute to this book, I was surprised how many came back to me, almost apologetically, saying that they had never travelled by bus to school – they had walked or, whisper it, had been taken in the family car. But as you will discover, there were many more who were keen to share their experiences of journeys by bus to school, and a few have also seen things from the other side and describe the problems of running buses for schoolchildren.

What is interesting are the common themes that emerge. Family cars were of course less common in the years when our contributors went to school, which cover the 1930s through to the 1970s; parents allowed children as young as five to travel alone to school; also, there appears to have been a resistance to organised games, often tempered only by the buses that took us to the sports fields or swimming baths; there was often creative use of bus timetables to 'chance' upon pupils from local girls' schools; and there are a few favourite routes, favourite buses, and even favourite conductors.

Buses will always play their part in getting children to and from school, whether they are crowding on to already busy commuter buses or travelling in dedicated buses, often with dedicated seats, American-style, as Sir Moir Lockhead has been actively championing for the UK.

Many of the photos that have been provided were taken at the time by contributors using the fairly basic cameras that were all we could afford. So, apologies if the photographic standard is not always what it could be; but it's the subject matter that is important.

The contributions are presented in purely alphabetical order to allow readers to enjoy a range of experiences that cover much of Britain, with a side-trip to Ireland as well.

From a personal point of view, it was trips to school by tram and then bus that attracted me to buses and into the bus industry and I have enjoyed reading the contributions from other well-known names that reveal how these early enthusiasms shaped their careers or hobbies.

Gavin Booth, Edinburgh

Silent, but for the swish of tyres

Michael H. C. Baker

Long-time enthusiast and transport author and photographer, recalls trolleybuses in London and Bournemouth

My earliest days were spent in a quiet, Croydon suburban street, which nevertheless possessed the priceless attribute of three London Transport tram routes and three bus routes, plus five Green Line ones passing along the London Road at the top of it, and another bus one passing along the Brighton Road at the other end. And to add even greater spice, not very far away, some ten minutes walk, was a trolleybus route. Being a child of World War II, model buses of any sort were quite unobtainable but my indulgent father painstakingly constructed a wooden one for Christmas 1943. He must have finished it late on Christmas Eve for the paint around the radiator was still slightly sticky when I found it in my pillowcase at the end of the bed next morning. Although of course I never mentioned it, I felt a slight sense of disappointment for its design was nothing like the STs and STLs with which I was familiar but with its protruding bonnet

The young Michael Baker in his very first conveyance on holiday in Weymouth 1938 aged one.

was an approximation of the pre-World War I B types that my father had grown up with.

My first school was a small preparatory one some two minutes walk away, just around the corner on the main road at which the headteacher, Mrs Edwards, asked us to pray for her son who whilst serving with the Eighth Army in North Africa had been captured by the Germans, and where the highlight of the week was a letter from Enid Blyton, printed in a weekly children's magazine. I also fell in love with Pamela, the head girl, aged 16.

It was Adolf Hitler who gave me my first regular experience of travelling to school by public transport. In early 1944 he directed a V1 on to the houses at the bottom of our garden, blowing off our roof and blowing out all the windows in the process, upon which we took ourselves off to Bournemouth where father worked for the NAAFI in a commandeered hotel on the clifftops, mum helped out in another hotel where I met and played on the beach with Lord Montgomery's nephew, and I went to school in Southbourne on a yellow Bournemouth no.25 trolleybus. War or not – and the town was awash with Americans heading for the Normandy beaches – Bournemouth was not going to let its standards slip and inside and outside its Sunbeam trolleys were always immaculate. I was mortified one afternoon when a school friend was admonished by the conductor for putting his feet on a seat. One distinctive feature of Bournemouth trolleybuses which they shared with the trams that passed the top of our road back home was the dual staircases, for going up and coming down.

Talking of which, the front door of the school was in Hampshire, the back door in Dorset, this being long before the county boundaries were changed, and each Wednesday afternoon – school, for some reason finished early that day – we would venture across the border to visit my grandmother who was staying for the duration with Uncle Will who owned a shoe shop in Poole High Street. This meant marching down to the town centre and joining a long queue inside the central bus station, most exciting, for proper, covered-in bus stations were quite outside my London Transport experiences – although during an earlier

Baker with the his dog Trix and the bus built by his dad.

evacuation, to Bognor Regis in 1940 I was greatly impressed by what I much later came to recognise as that town's handsome, and now much missed, art deco establishment. Hants & Dorset operated four frequent routes between Bournemouth and Poole so that if the first bus was full it was no great disaster and we usually managed to find an upstairs seat on the next one, a seat designed for four not very large people, up into which one climbed from the sunken side gangway. This was another experience to savour; no doubt the adults much preferred the greater comfort of the trolleybuses which, however, did not penetrate into Poole, although the trams they had replaced some 10 or so years before had done. It would have

One of Bournemouth Corporation's 1935 vintage Sunbeam MS2/Park Royal trolleybuses at the Square.

been possible to travel to school by Hants & Dorset bus, for the Poole routes traversed the same road as the 25 trolleybuses as far as Southbourne, where the trolleys terminated on a loop around the shops whilst the buses drew up alongside a rather fetching rustic bus shelter at County Gates before venturing into deepest Dorset, but I don't think I ever did, not least because the buses always seemed to be full to capacity: apart from which a trolleybus was somehow rather more exotic.

Although Hants & Dorset, as a Tilling Company, had begun to buy Bristols just before the war the Bournemouth to Poole routes must have been operated by their immediate predecessors, TD3 and TD4 Leyland Titans, for sometimes on summer evenings before going to sleep I would listen to the sound of a bus toiling up the steep hill out of the town towards Poole, a sound identical to that which I recalled from my Bognor days when we travelled on

Southdown routes 31 and 50, always operated by Leyland Titans. That particular throaty, subdued but purposeful roar was and is one of the most evocative sounds I've ever experienced, along with the distinctive click of the garden gate of my Aunt Agnes's cottage in Shropshire and, vastly less pleasant, the wail of the air-raid siren which brought us out of our beds and scurrying down to the Anderson shelter at the end of the garden.

Whilst any trolleybus of my acquaintance has always claimed to be virtually silent, I have always associated two distinct noises with such vehicles which take me instantly back to 1944-45 in Bournemouth, one the swish of the tyres, particularly as they took the curves around the Square, the hub of the network, the other the drumming and boom on the roof as, slowing to a magisterial and dignified pace, their poles negotiated the overhead wiring junctions.

It might have been different if all buses had been the same

Harry L. Barker

Enthusiast and author, remembers schoolday journeys from East Lothian into Edinburgh

I was brought up in Pencaitland, an attractive East Lothian village with a population of around 700 on the edge of the East Lothian coalfield about 15 miles – or to be precise 46 minutes – by bus from Edinburgh.

My late father had attended one of Edinburgh's famous schools – The Royal High – famous partly because it educated Sir Walter Scott, and other less noble students (some considerably less so!), but High Scholars always tended to regard themselves as 'special'

and usually wanted their sons (it was an all-boys school) to follow in their footsteps. So at the tender age of nine my twin brother and I were duly dispatched to the Royal High for the remainder of our school years. Sir Walter Scott may have long departed when I commenced my classical education in 1960, but I do recall the late Robin Cook, later to serve in Tony Blair's administration and whose father made a brave but largely unsuccessful attempt to teach me chemistry.

Now our cottage was situated less than

100 yards from the village bus terminus and there were 29 journeys a day that terminated there or passed the house. From now on I was to sample the delights of these mechanical wonders. Having had to listen to all sorts of tales of operational catastrophe from my father who used the buses daily to get to work in Edinburgh, the prospect was potentially exciting. At that time the first bus, and the only really suitable one, left the village at 07.34am arriving in Edinburgh at 08.20am, soon enough to allow us to get to school on time. We had to cross the busy A1 road at a traffic island but in these days this was no great deal for a nine year old. The bus was very busy and by the next village a duplicate was provided and both buses were full to standing, then merged with other services the closer we got to Edinburgh and a convoy of perhaps eight or more buses from various points proceeded in what seemed a serious and frantic dash to work – different from a stroll in a country village to school.

It took less than a week for me to notice that all buses were not the same – and even if today's was similar to yesterday's the fleet number would probably be different,

Resting at Edinburgh bus station before a trip to Pencaitland, a 1970 Bristol LH6P with Alexander Y type body that had come to Eastern Scottish from Highland Omnibuses but had been new to Alexander (Midland).
Harry L. Barker collection

signifying a different bus from the same batch, or even a different year. Some were underfloor-engined – by far the better, or so I thought at the time – and others had the engine at the front. All were single-deckers in the morning, but occasionally a double-decker would appear in the afternoon. I gradually got to know the rough extent of the fleet, their registration numbers (and was therefore able to identify the year of manufacture of all other locally-registered road vehicles), and fathom out the fleet numbering system, including the depot codes. At this time there were no fleetbooks to tell me what was going on and that made life even more exciting. Because the bus company – Scottish Omnibuses Ltd (but known even to this day as SMT) – was based in

Scottish Omnibuses had many of its AEC Regals rebodied with full-front Burlingham Seagull coach bodies in the 1950s. The door that Bertie Smith mistook for the entrance is above the nearside front wheel in this view of a 1949 Regal III with 1954 body in St Andrew Square, Edinburgh.
Harry L. Barker collection

The Pencaitland service attracted some more unusual buses in the Eastern Scottish fleet, like this 1957 AEC Regent V/Massey, acquired with the business of Baxter, Airdrie in 1962. *Harry L. Barker collection*

Edinburgh, new buses would appear annually on our routes before they were allocated to other depots in the Borders, or across the central belt of Scotland to Airdrie and Glasgow.

I marvelled at the complexity of the timetable for our five local routes and the ingenious way timings interlinked with each other and connecting services to Berwick-upon-Tweed and Newcastle. My geography became significantly better as I knew where all the buses went and by studying the route map a whole new hobby emerged, including the operational and mechanical aspects, and photography.

Of course some incidents stand out to this day – such as one Bertie Smith who boarded a front-engined AEC Regal rebodied with a full-front Burlingham Seagull coach body, its entrance being situated behind the front wheel rather than at the very front as on an underfloor-engined bus. The design of the body camouflaged the door and Bertie climbed through a small door above the nearside front wheel into the engine compartment and only realised something was wrong when he was unable to get through the glass on the front bulkhead into the passenger saloon. The crew were in stitches. Then there were the notices in the bus 'TO SEAT 35 PASSENGERS' or 'SPITTING PROHIBITED' duly altered by wags to 'TO EAT 35 PASSENGERS' or 'SITTING PROHIBITED' using a penknife to erase the S or P. Then there was the driver who approached a stop too close on a double-decker and walloped a lamp-post with a thud, thud, thud along the window panes.

A later view illustrating the difficulties sometimes faced by commuters from more rural areas, a 1978 Eastern Scottish Seddon Pennine 7/Alexander heads for Pencaitland in heavy snow. *Harry L. Barker*

He immediately jumped out his cab and tried to throw me off the bus as he thought I had been stamping my feet immediately above his head, as I was upstairs at the front – schoolboys were always suspected, usually wrongly, of being troublemakers. Some misguided conductresses (rarely conductors) would not even let me upstairs and would then complain if I did not get up to stand for adults. I would explain that I had wanted to go upstairs, and had she allowed me to, I would not be taking up the seat and I refused as a result. There were usually empty seats upstairs.

My journeys to school were indeed exciting and today they have given me a hobby that means that wherever I go in the world, there are always buses to be seen – some unknown to me and many more that are familiar or their origin can be guessed at. I am never bored; just put me on a bus or let me walk the streets with a camera and I am happy to record and see what is going on. There is always something new, not always a bus, but a route change or a livery.

Today schoolchildren regard buses as litter-bins, boxing rings and a hideaway from parents and schoolteachers. Many never travel on a bus to school, as their mothers (usually) take them by car creating all sorts of mayhem, and a direct result of policies not to provide free transport for those living two or three miles from school. What a pity only a few will ever experience the world of discovery and excitement and provide themselves with a hobby for life.

Avoiding sport and discovering girls

Gavin Booth

Writer and passenger champion, on a Scottish childhood that encouraged his interest in transport

Life would all have been so different if my parents had sent me to the local corporation school, just a short walk away. Instead they chose to send me to a school that was a couple of miles away and thus beyond walking distance for a five year old. Instead of developing an interest in buses as a result of these daily journeys I might well have turned out to be a sporting star. But then again, maybe not.

Gavin and wee sister Sheila at Morecambe in 1949. If Gavin had noticed the bus behind, surely he would have chosen that.

Instead of sending me to Towerbank Primary and Portobello High – where I am sure I would have received a perfectly good education, let me say – I was sent to Edinburgh's Royal High School, a school where my father and sundry uncles had gone before me. I started at the Preparatory School in 1948, some two miles from my Joppa home, and in 1955 I moved to the 'big school', the iconic Grecian-styled school building in the city

Eastfield terminus with the Firth of Forth on the right. Sister Sheila would have got the nasty Edinburgh Corporation Northern Counties-rebodied wartime Guy Arab on the right to get to Leith Academy on the 25, but Gavin would have used the splendid Leyland Titan/Metro-Cammell Orion on the left, on the 26. *Gavin Booth*

centre, on the slopes of Calton Hill. This was even further from Joppa, so for virtually every day of my 13 years at Royal High I travelled by Edinburgh Corporation bus – actually tram until November 1954.

The Royal High was a sort of hybrid at the time, a corporation fee-paying school. In a city where the school you attended tends to indicate your place on the social ladder, Royal High was neither a true corporation school nor one of the rather more expensive private fee-paying schools. The Royal High fees were nothing like as expensive as those for the private schools but there was the expense of a very exactly specified school uniform and my parents had to buy all my school books.

After six years of travelling by tram (which, whisper it in a book about bus journeys to school, encouraged my love of trams) Edinburgh Corporation buses took over and these carried me to school and indeed everywhere around the city. The Booth family didn't have a car until the late 1950s so every journey was a journey of discovery. The buses on the 26 route that replaced the trams were Metro-Cammell Orion-bodied Leyland Titan PD2/20s, buses I have often written about over the past half-century. That they were skimpily-finished lightweights didn't matter a jot to me; they were brand-new and, with their tin fronts, undoubtedly 'modern'. The fact that they

Eastfield again with Seaview Terrace on the left and the Booth residence just out of sight behind one of Edinburgh Corporation's 11 unpainted Leyland PD2/Orions, looking just a bit scruffy by this time. *Gavin Booth*

were clearly inferior to the well-finished buses that Edinburgh had previously bought was of no real concern to me at the age of 11. For the rest of my schooldays the Orions would be standard fare on the 26, though as the 26 was a good performer it received newer buses at regular intervals so we got progressively younger buses from the batch of Orions that would number 300, including briefly the 10 unpainted examples that represented the last deliveries in 1957.

The trip took 10 minutes to the Preparatory School and 20 minutes to the 'big school' so I had the chance to get to know these buses well. I lived fairly near Eastfield terminus so I often walked there to catch my bus, assuring me of the front upstairs offside seat and, when there was a chance of something different, a choice of

buses, assuming I wasn't running late. There were regular short-workings on the 26, often just to Waverley, a couple of stops past the big school, and these were operated by some of the older buses from Central Garage. These included the former London Transport Guys with newer Duple Nudd bodies, or the big batch of Birmingham-style Daimler/Metro-Cammells, or one of the Brockhouse-bodied AEC Regent IIIs that never quite fitted into the fleet – or even, joy of joys, an all-Leyland Titan PD2/12 from my all-time favourite batch.

I didn't have a favourite individual bus, in the same way that I had a favourite engine from my previous trainspotting days (A1 Pacific No 60142 *Edward Fletcher* if you want to know), but I do remember I had a favourite conductor, who was always friendly

The only time Gavin took a tram to the 'big school', the splendid Grecian-style building on the left, was for swimming lessons. This is a 1934 Edinburgh Corporation-built standard on the 20 back to Joppa.

Buses like this 1946 Guy Arab II/Northern Counties always seemed crude and noisy to the young Gavin, especially when compared with his beloved Leylands. This 26 is only going to Kings Road, so Gavin would have let it pass unless he was feeling energetic.

and chatty, in contrast to the conductors and conductresses who always grunted at schoolkids.

There was a downside to going to the Royal High rather than Portobello High: no girls. Royal High was a boys' school while Portobello was co-ed, so the 'Porty' boys were relaxed and confident with girls, while those of us at single-sex schools were just a wee bit awkward. Not that this stopped me from attempting to charm the local girls, but I found that the girls I related best to went to girls' schools, which was fine. The girls' schools were in or near the city centre and the girls too had to travel by the 26. I recall with some embarrassment that I occasionally caught my bus to school at stops that were nowhere near my house but were near theirs.

There was always the chance of something a bit different on the 26, like this 1943 Daimler CWG5 with 1954 Alexander body, here in Princes Street.

The 'Television Train' to Pitlochry gave Gavin the chance to photograph the first Alexander one-man bus, Leyland Tiger PA66. Gavin Booth

The Royal High had no playing-fields near the big school so we were bundled on to buses to take us to Jock's Lodge for rugby or Holyrood for cricket. That was unless I had a note. Which was often.

The buses used were provided of course by Edinburgh Corporation and tended to be the oldest buses in the fleet. I well remember a trip in no.27, a 1937 Daimler COG6/Metro-Cammell double-decker, one of the last of the big prewar Daimler fleet. I hadn't quite sussed out how the fleet was numbered, but I guessed that such a low fleet number meant an old bus. And on this occasion I was right.

I realised that this assumption was highly flawed when the first Tiger Cubs arrived in 1959, numbered 1 to 50. I think *Buses Illustrated* had helped me to understand the numbering of the newer buses in the fleet, in the absence of anything else, but because Edinburgh Corporation was apparently

buying buses in batches of 50 or 100 at the time, it seemed natural to me that bus companies always bought batches in round numbers, at least. So my attempts at fleet lists in the late 1950s suggest that Edinburgh had more buses than it actually owned. Like 20 of these Regent IIIs (there were 17), or 20 Northern Counties-bodied Guy Arab IIIs (there were 15) or more than 21 all-Leyland PD2s, mainly because I had seen number 240 as well as 260 and couldn't believe they would start a numbering scheme at 240 rather than 241; but of course they had, and there were just 21. Much later when the corporation's successor, Lothian, started batches at round numbers (300, 800) I was told that the engineers were to blame; maybe they were in the 1950s too.

Eventually I managed to get a fleet list from Edinburgh Corporation and this splendid and much-treasured document was a multi-page internal document that gave every conceivable detail about every bus, including dates of delivery, chassis numbers and dates when buses were rebuilt.

The big school was a short walk from Princes Street and a slightly longer walk to the corporation's Central Garage at Annandale Street. So while my Porty friends were standing on street corners chatting up Porty girls after school I was sneaking round Central Garage to see what was there. I was always law-abiding so was very reluctant to trespass and risk being shouted at. Occasionally an inspector would take pity and escort me round the garage, but usually I was standing at the door straining to see what was inside. There was a side door that wasn't used by buses but was usually open and any new buses tended to be parked near there after delivery; if there was something really exciting, I would throw caution to the wind and rush in, take a look, memorise the number, and dash outside again. That was when I wasn't conspiring to just happen to be at a Princes Street bus stop when the current object of my teenage lust was on her way home.

We didn't seem to have many away-days from school, though I do recall one – the 'Television Train' to Pitlochry. In the days when we could still get excited by television, this was a train with what must have been a crude form of CCTV where we sat and had lessons as we proceeded north from Edinburgh through the countryside. What made it worthwhile for me was the discovery of what was then, I think, the only one-man-operated bus in the Alexander fleet – maybe in the whole Scottish Bus Group – 1948 Leyland Tiger PS1/Alexander no.PA66, which I photographed enthusiastically.

Our house in Seaview Terrace, Joppa was good for buses. From the front upstairs window we could see Eastfield terminus and the appearance of something new or rare would prompt a sharp exit from the house.

We also had Scottish Omnibuses services passing the house, usually at some speed as SOL drivers were reluctant to pick up passengers within the boundary – 'scratchers' – and would drive by an outstretched hand even when there were plenty of seats available.

The SOL buses were interesting, but there were lots of AECs. I had decided that if Leylands were good enough for Edinburgh Corporation Transport Manager Moris Little, then they were certainly good enough for me. In fact Edinburgh Corporation became and stayed my favourite operator.

So when I left school and started looking for a job I applied at Edinburgh Corporation but thought I had better approach Scottish Omnibuses just in case. The job I took was at Scottish Omnibuses, based at New Street, below and within sight of the Royal High School. So I continued making much the same journey as I had to get to school, occasionally managing to flag down a speeding SOL AEC Monocoach to make use of my Privilege Ticket. But mainly I stuck to the 26.

There were other boys at Royal High who turned out to be vaguely interested in buses, but not many. Later the Barker twins travelled into the school from Pencaitland – see Harry Barker's contribution in this book – and I got to know Richard Iles, who went on to a successful career in transport. But they were younger than me, so I missed the chance to do a bit of gricing with them – not that we called it gricing at the time; bus-spotting, probably.

I enjoyed the Royal High, a school full of history and character where you were a god if you were in the first fifteen or the first eleven but you were regarded as slightly weird if you were interested in trains or even buses. But those daily trips to and from school and the proximity of the city centre helped to fashion the rest of my life.

Mind you, if I had gone to Porty …

The long walk, a first kiss and the decorated bus shelter ...

Andrew Braddock

Transport consultant, magazine columnist and formerly a senior bus company manager, discovers buses and girls in the West Country

It would be unthinkable today. No parent would countenance such a thing. That mile-and-a-quarter walk from the bus to the train. Come rain or shine, each morning I trudged that great distance from Charlton Road station to the Cenotaph in Shepton Mallet, Somerset, from age 11 to 14 to reach Wells Cathedral School. In the afternoons it could be avoided as a bus-to-bus connection at said Cenotaph was usually available, choir practice permitting.

Though I was born near Highgate underground station in North London, my family moved twice in my formative years – firstly to Ickenham (then practically a suburb of Uxbridge, still in Middlesex) and later to Evercreech in the heart of the Mendip Hills. Now walking to and from school was the norm in those far-off days and I can just about remember being passed by red London Transport RTs on the daily trot along Swakeleys Road, and the joys of shopping trips to Uxbridge to catch sight of green Country Area RTs and RFs, with the latter the mainstay of Green Line Coaches, of course. My favourite trip was to an Aunt in Hayes on a 607 trolleybus and these seemingly huge three-axle leviathans had taken my fancy on the Archway Road as my earliest bus memories.

So, at age seven, to the West Country – and certainly a different world as far as public transport was concerned. My father was a retail pharmacist and his shop (with our house adjoining) had a perfect view of the bus stops outside the village hall from which Wake's Services and Western National plied their trade. To a Londoner with more than a passing interest in buses and trains it took a while, I suppose, to get used to blue double-

LYA 449, one of the 'pair of magnificent AECs' used by Wake's Services of Sparkford, Yeovil – a Regent III with Reading body on which Andrew Braddock travelled on the Shepton Mallet service.

deckers with no route number and green single-deckers with a door at the back rather than the front. When I first went to Shepton Mallet on the bus with my mother I found the four-abreast seating of Wake's lowbridge AECs very strange! I had not got round to RLHs in London (few and far between as they were) so the sunken gangway and 'mind your head when leaving your seat' exhortations on the lower deck offside seemed distinctly odd.

As for the trains – well, there's many a rail fan would happily have killed for the chance to live by the Somerset & Dorset Joint Railway. 'Swift & Delightful' to its friends (there were few) and 'Slow & Dirty' to the agnostic majority, this iconic line was indeed a veritable treasure. Ancient locomotives of Midland Railway origin were still responsible for most local passenger trains through Evercreech New (opened in 1874), wheezing and leaking steam from every orifice as they struggled up the northbound 1 in 50 gradient while taking yours truly the one stop to Shepton when my Wells schooldays began.

But it's the buses I am supposed to be reminiscing about here. They were lovely too – especially the pair of magnificent AECs of Wake's with bodywork by Reading of Portsmouth (to a Duple design I would say). If I recall correctly they were LYA 449 and LYB 113 and LYA appears in my 'Box Brownie' photograph here. This pair were the mainstay of the lengthy Yeovil to Shepton Mallet service, though occasionally a Duple-bodied AEC Reliance coach would appear instead – I think this was TYB 888 or similar. I am pretty sure the Regent IIIs had LT-style preselect gearboxes because I can remember drivers complaining when they were joined by an ex-Bristol Omnibus K5G a few years after I started travelling on the service.

Western National's contribution to Evercreech life was initially Bristol L type halfcabs and later LSs on the 211/228, which meandered from Glastonbury to Bruton though not really in serious competition with Wake's. My regular school run was by train in the morning, followed by a Lodekka on Bristol's 43A to Wells (occasionally substituted with a lowbridge KSW) but on most days I managed an all-bus return home via Wake's or WN depending on the time. I recall that the Blue School boys (and girls) used the train from Shepton to Wells (the ex-Great Western Cheddar Valley branch) whereas us Cathedral School boys (we had no girls, I'm afraid) went by bus, though it was not uncommon for us to swap season tickets and go by the forbidden mode!

Apart from those memories of the buses (which I was interested in, of course) there's the memory of Sally Treasure too (and I was most certainly interested in her). Sometime in my thirteenth year I savoured the experience of a first 'proper' kiss with the good Sally in the double seat at the rear of the top-deck of a 43A Lodekka, which led to us 'going out' for a while. This usually meant meeting in Shepton on a Saturday night to go to the cinema, with me taking the last Wake's bus home. It didn't last I'm afraid, but at least a bus had brought us together!

Oh, and the decorated shelter? In the run-up to Christmas one year a bunch of mates and I purloined a few ticket rolls from the 43A conductor's box one afternoon and spread them artistically around the shelter at Dinder on the way out of Wells. There was help at hand from a couple of local lads who brought toilet rolls from a nearby pub to finish the job. The whole ensemble was there for all to see next morning, but afternoon winds blew the lot away!

'Don't use the trolleybus'

Geoff Burrows

Classic Bus magazine's fount of knowledge, on discoveries and warnings in 1930s South Shields

Buses were little brown things that took mother and I to grandfather's shop in Laygate. We lived in Cleadon Park, South Shields in a new privately-run housing estate in the early 1930s. Since being made redundant from a shipyard office job, father had set up a little printing shop in his garden shed. To reach his customers and suppliers he bought a 1928 Austin 7, the only car in our street at the time. Father never used this for school journeys, whatever the weather, or even to take mother to the shops.

One day I was walking home with mother when a gleaming blue single-decker roared past. 'What's that, mother?' 'It's a corporation bus.' 'Then what are the little brown things?' 'They're corporation buses, too,' she replied. Now this didn't satisfy my three-year-old enquiring mind because all she had to say was 'it's a Daimler COG5 with Weymann body,' but she didn't. It took me years to find out, and by then I was hooked.

In 1935 I started school, this meant a 20-minute walk there and back in the morning and evening. At lunch time, or 'dinner time' as this was the north-east, we walked a short distance from the school to the 'car stop' in Prince Edward Road. There we waited for the four or five 'workmen's' buses that rushed up from the shipyards on the riverside bringing the workers home for their dinners. Some usually went by full but one or two always stopped for us to board. We paid our ha'penny fares, and arrived home in time for a proper meal before walking back to school. We used this arrangement because the normal service buses were inconvenient in time and distance from school.

These dinner-time buses were a mixture of old and new. Some were 'brown', but larger than the ones that I have already mentioned, and occasionally one of the two-year-old blue ones would show up. Then there were what we christened the 'new blue-ies'. To my by now practised eye these were old 'brown' buses repainted blue, but later there were a couple of different ones in new blue paint. We soon leant to avoid these because as soon

'A Little Brown Thing' – one of the South Shields Morris Commercial 14-seaters with Davidson body.
Geoff Burrows collection.

A South Shields 'new Blue-ie', a 1928 AEC Reliance that came from Northern General in 1937, that was new to Eastern Express of West Hartlepool in 1928. It is seen here outside Readhead's shipyard waiting for the 'dinner time dash.' *Geoff Burrows collection.*

as they reached the hill near home they spluttered and backfired in their struggle to climb the far from steep gradient. If there was a Daimler in the convoy, it would roar past, to the shouts and jeers of us children.

One day as we stood waiting at the car stop we noticed that pairs of tall poles were being planted along the road. They could have been lamp-posts but they looked suspiciously like the poles holding the tram wires in King George Road. 'They're for the new trolleybuses,' explained father. 'A waste of money, you'll see.' As the weeks went by, the system grew. First the span wires were put between the pairs of poles. Then the running wires were tied to these, one at a time. Gradually the fittings were all put together and the wires properly attached.

Now I knew what trolleybuses were; I had seen them while on family visits to Darlington and Teesside. So I confidently explained to my friends that they would be single-deckers, like all the other South Shields buses at that time. So imagine my shock when one day a magnificent blue double-decker trolleybus appeared with one man driving and another in the cab teaching him. This happened every day for a few weeks – oddly they came in opposite directions on each succeeding day.

Then came the great day when the trolleybus service began: Monday 12 October 1936. Father gave strict instructions that we were not to use them. As we waited at our usual stop only one single-deck bus along came, not three or four – and it went straight past, full. Panic! We looked down the road and there was a trolleybus on its way. It stopped, and we all piled on, though it was already full. The conductor squeezed through taking our ha'pennies as we listened in awe to the intermittent clicking sounds coming from the driver's cab and the lack of engine noise. As the speed increased a loud rumble picked up under the floor, making everything vibrate. We got off at the new Freemantle Road terminus where the wires ended in a turning loop. A short walk home – and father was livid! 'I told you not to use those things, they've made you late.' It did no good telling him that there were no buses anyway.

The same procedure followed for the next few days, then the dinner-time journeys returned to normal, by motorbus, and peace reigned again. Apparently the trolleybuses were intended to replace the motorbus route entirely but they didn't go near enough to the shipyards, so the workmen's buses were reinstated. The regular service was also put back but it no longer followed what was now the trolleybus route to Laygate; instead it took a longer route round the town. So to father's disgust we had to use the trolleybus to go to grandfather's shop. Not only that, but they were hugely successful, and always full.

The old brown buses disappeared as did the 'new blue-ies,' replaced by real new buses. In 1938 new double-deckers with forward entrances began to replace the single-deckers, which were switched to augment the Simonside route and to introduce new services.

Autumn 1939 brought great changes to our lives. We were moved to a newly-built school, and the war began. The journey to school was about the same distance but no bus routes went anywhere near. So it meant

walking all the way, but of course we were older and bigger now.

In 1941 I was awarded a scholarship to the High School, which was further away and again nowhere near a bus route. However I had been rewarded with a bicycle, so no problem.

The war took its toll on the town, with heavy bombing, and cost the lives of many merchant seamen from Shields in the Atlantic U-boat attacks. Many buses were borrowed to carry the additional passengers to and from the places of work revitalised by war production. So in addition to the strange shapes and makes of the visitors from London, Leeds, Manchester, Newcastle and

Now fully restored to original condition, South Shields no.204 was one of 34 Karrier E4s operated, the largest quantity of the type with any operator. All had near-identical Weymann bodies. No.204 can be seen at the Sandtoft Trolleybus Museum. *Gavin Booth*

Another of the Karrier E4/Weymann trolleybuses in the South Shields fleet. *Ian Allan Library*

Sunderland, there were the new utility buses. But that, as they say, is another story.

As I grew older, my knowledge of the South Shields buses increased and I can fill in the gaps for the reader. There were four 'little brown things', Morris Commercial 14-seaters built in 1925, CU 1757-60. The bigger brown buses were Guy BAs CU 1915-17; Guy BBs CU 1993-4 and CU 2076-7; and Guy FBB CU 2568; all were built between 1926 and 1929 with Guy bodies. The Daimler COG5s were CU 3204-7 with Weymann bodies (1934); CU 3417-9 with Willowbrook bodies (1935); CU 3569-70, 3793 with NCB bodies (1936/37). The 'new blue-ies' were 1928/29 AEC Reliances, EF 3985 and FT 1929 that came from Northern General. The double-deckers were again Daimler COG5s with Weymann forward entrance bodies, CU 3980-2, 4188-9, new 1938.

The trolleybuses also favoured Weymann bodies, on Karrier E4 chassis with Met-Vick electrical equipment. The motors were fitted right at the front to give a low floor line to reduce height for the many railway bridges. Consequently the propeller shaft was very long, and they 'whipped' considerably until modifications were made later.

My school bus journeys only spanned three years – but then I did ride on one of the first South Shields trolleybuses on the first day of service.

Character-forming in Cornwall

Brian Cox

Describes the school journeys in Cornwall, Berkshire and Sussex that may have led him into a distinguished transport career

I was the archetypal child for whose school journey the phrase 'integrated transport' could have been invented. It was my father's fault: he was a horticulturalist, always with a tied house, rarely near a bus route even in the 1950s and 1960s of what people rather frighteningly now call 'the last century'. Or my mother's: she always wanted the best for me, to send me to the better school. My sister, younger, hasn't got over this 'favouritism' yet, 50-odd years later. The better school, of course, was always more difficult to get to, didn't have a direct bus and took ages to get there. On reflection, perhaps they just wanted me out of the house as long as possible: I expect I was a big-headed brat. No comments required, thank you very much! They couldn't afford to send me to boarding school, which would have solved everyone's problems nicely.

So, at the age of seven or so, in the mid-1950s, living on the estate of Antony House (now National Trust) outside Torpoint in Cornwall, I was sent as a day boy to Plymouth College Prep School: in my father's Austin 7 (CLN 594, almost the only car number plate I can remember) up to the main road, then the green Western National bus to Torpoint Ferry, over the ferry as a foot passenger to Devonport, and then the red Plymouth Corporation bus up to somewhere near, but not very near, the school, because I remember a long uphill walk at the end (but not always, so perhaps there was more than one bus route). Even now I have vague memories of fear of missing the bus and I

Below: The young Brian with sister Marilyn and dog Gyp.

Bottom: Brian caught the Western National bus to Torpoint to catch the ferry to Plymouth. There he would encounter buses like this 1947 Western National Leyland Titan PD1A with ECW body. *Ian Allan Library*

think it was connected with the ferry and the red buses, so it fits in. It's a wonder I didn't start smoking then (that came later). Anyway, I'm sure it was very character-forming.

Then (after an interlude in Worcester) it was the bus from Shinfield to Reading (Thames Valley – or was it Reading Corporation?) and then the electric train from Reading South to school at Winnersh. I don't remember the buses but I do the old Southern Region 2BIL and 2HAL electric units, and the very occasional homeward steam journey behind an N or U Class Mogul if one of the Guildford line trains happened to get halted by the signals at Winnersh.

And, finally, a bus that I *can* remember, the good old Southdown Queen Mary, the first flat-fronted double-decker I can ever remember seeing and still the only bus I ever really feel nostalgic about. Thanks to my mother again, I should add: she insisted I went to Chichester rather than Worthing High School, because it was said to be better. So instead of a simple train journey to Worthing, it was the Queen Mary to Littlehampton and then the familiar SR electrics of my Reading days over to Chichester.

Perhaps I was destined for a career in transport: I seem to have experienced enough of it.

Buses encountered in Reading would have included corporation AEC Regent III/Park Royal buses or all-Crossley DD42/7s like the bus second on the left. All are built to lowbridge layout, which was standard across the Reading motorbus fleet at the time.

Smoke-filled trolleybuses and empty school buses

Roger Davies

Former bus company manager and now consultant and columnist, on travelling to school in Cardiff and running school buses in various parts of the NBC empire

I first encountered school in Cardiff. I grew up at Victoria Park and my first school was a short walk along Cowbridge Road. At that time it was served by no fewer than 32 trolleybuses an hour, some motorbuses and exotic beasts from the likes of Western Welsh

and Neath & Cardiff. It's a wonder I could cross the road. But the constant presence must have made an impact.

My high school, from 1961, was a bit further along in Canton requiring use of these conveyances. I well recall smoke-filled upper

Start of many a journey to Canton High and the point from which 32 trolleybuses an hour headed towards Cardiff City centre was Victoria Park terminus, also very close to Roger's home. In June 1966, long after the High School had fled to Fairwater, East Lancs-bodied BUT no.222 waits to head off to the Royal Oak on the other side of the city. It was unique in being the only one of 55 dual-doorway trolleybuses dating from 1948 to 1950 not to have its front door panelled over as you can see in this shot. A 1955 BUT heads out to Ely across the road adorned with a classic Cardiff beer advert painted on in fleet livery. Not much interest to a schoolkid. Yet.

decks of trolleybuses, the ceilings that awful nicotine shade of yellow/brown with condensation-streaming windows. Their warm, damp atmosphere often provided haven for last-minute swotting for tests. It's a wonder I remember them with such fondness. The return journey required waiting at a typical Cardiff trolley stop, a stencilled note on a traction pole, from which you could see approaching buses appear around a distant corner. I used to stun my friends by recognising the advancing bus by its paintwork or adverts.

After a year, the school was moved to the outer suburbs in Fairwater. The old building still exists as an arts centre and is a regular in the Good Beer Guide, endowing it with more fondness than it deserves. The new site was a whole different kettle of fish requiring use of the hitherto rare breed for me – motorbuses. In fairness to the school, they enquired of our new travel arrangements and my 'walk across the park and get a 31, 32B or 50 at Chargot Road' was deemed acceptable. 'Was it nice?' they asked.

After the move to Fairwater Roger's bus journey home finished here in Chargot Road where 1956 Daimler CVG6/East Lancs no.308 stops on the notable date of 6/6/66. Roger caught the bus to school at the stop on the left; it was the bit after the buses between these two stops he didn't overly like.

The exciting Cardiff no.426 seen when a bit older in October 1966 – if a Guy Arab V with East Lancs body can be exciting at any time. It's in the bus station heading off to places I never visited, but never mind. Actually, it is quite nice. But not exciting.

This opened up all manner of wonders. Cardiff's bus fleet at the time was hugely varied and anything, a Daimler, Guy, AEC, Bristol or Leyland with a goodly variety of bodywork could swing around the corner. The 1950 Regent IIIs, particular favourites, were still so highly thought of they worked the lengthy 50 regularly. Then one day, out of the 1962 gloom came brand-new Regent V no.383 all aglow with fluorescent lights, Formica-backed seats and a translucent roof panel. I still think of it as the height of modernity.

The girls were on site too although the intervening no-mans-land was equipped with high fences, machine gun posts, razor wire – you know, the usual sort of thing. They were let out early to get on the buses first, irritating but as time and the girls developed I grew to forgive. We used to get round it by nipping out of the back of the school (which was actually the front but as we came in at the back we thought of it as the back not the front; that was the back, if you follow) to get to the stop before the girls' one.

The journey though was walkable and, very early in 1965 as I ambled along Fairwater Road a brand-new bus hove into sight. Cardiff was taking in 17 Guy Arab Vs with East Lancs bodies, the slow delivery of which I think turned once-loyal CCT away from that bodybuilder. Five long and three short ones had arrived bearing Cardiff's first year-

The Willowbrook PD3 on which Roger was petrified by schoolkids at Etwall, Trent no.587 in Uttoxeter New Road, Derby, near Trent's head office, in January 1974. He forgave the bus, driving it many a time, finding it wonderful. As bus crews today still claim schoolkids are the scariest of passengers, perhaps if we actually got round to solving this long-standing problem, there would be far-reaching consequences for all.

suffix registrations, ABO-B. The new one headed towards me, no.426, was ABO 426C, my first experience of the suffix changing with the year. Look, I know it sounds inconsequential, but, as the registration system then, for a brief four years, actually made sense, it was quite something.

I spent some time with CCT and one day after a route change where we had turned terminating services into circulars, I got a call from an agitated mum. Apparently every day she put her son on the bus at the last but one stop, the bus turned around and she waved as son passed by. Today the bus plus boy had turned left and disappeared. 'Never fear,' I said, 'it'll be in town soon, I'll get the lad and send him home.' A quick check elicited that the bus was due to leave in four minutes from halfway across the city so without a word I dashed out. Gasping and panting, I just caught the conductor as his finger was about to press the bell, but a quick search revealed no schoolboy. I staggered back to the office to be told 'a lady rang for you, says the boy got off at the next stop and walked back home'.

I then went to college in Sheffield. The tales from here and the fabulous buses really need a 'buses and students' article of their own. Thus, gorgeous Park Royal Regent Vs on the 97, Fleetlines climbing all the way from the city to Crookes on the 52 and all

manner of things on the 1, 17, 24 and 63 along Abbeydale Road will have to wait for another time.

After a stint at Western Welsh where I'm sure we must have carried schoolkids but they never crossed my path, I arrived at Trent. Here I was taught to conduct and drive but union restrictions on when I could work tended to keep me away from school times. I did conduct one school bus, one of the many from Etwall school. We had a Willowbrook PD3 so I was on my own. I cowered on the platform gazing out of the back window for the whole journey absolutely terrified.

Etwall School provided a further incident. I was driving an 18 Tutbury back to Derby one dark and murky night. I had a dual-purpose Leopard 49-seater, no.247, and we had about a dozen guests on board. As we dipped into Etwall at about 8pm, the entire place seemed full of schoolkids, there must have been some event. There was a Blue Bus service, but neither the conductor nor I knew when but we did know there wasn't another 18 for an hour. We agreed we couldn't leave them out here. I pulled up, opened the door and looked the other way, feeling no.247 sink beneath me. Off we set, with me having to constantly clear the windscreen. The conductor reported he sold 72 tickets and some had returns. Eyebrows will

Bowland Bridge in March 1976 and Ribble Leopard no.683 (formerly no.458) turns outside the post office. Happily, said post office still survives in early 2009, aided by a lovely little cafe famous for its ever-changing soup of the day. The bus is typical of such vehicles in the area including Flookborough baths contracts.

| Service 540 | KENDAL · BOWLAND BRIDGE via Underbarrow, Crosthwaite | Table |
| Service 541 | KENDAL . WINDERMERE via Crook, Bowness | A |

Mondays to Fridays only

Service No.	540 ⊕	540 †	541	540	540 WF	540 ⊕
KENDAL, Bus Stn., Blackhall Road ....dep	0710	0738	0900	1315	1605	1745
Crook, Sun Inn.................... ,,	....	....	0915	1330	1618	1800
Crook, Wild Boar Inn .... ,,	*	*	0922	....	1625	....
Crook, Sun Inn.................... ,,	....	....	....	1330	1632	1800
Underbarrow, Punch Bowl .... ,,	0726	0754	....	1341	1643	1811
Crosthwaite, Post Office .... ,,	0733	0801	....	1348	1650	1818
BOWLAND BRIDGE, Post Office......arr	0740	....	....	....	1657	....
Bowness, Kendal Bank Rd. Corner....dep	....	....	0930	....	....	....
Baddeley Clock........................ ,,	....	....	0934	....	....	....
WINDERMERE, Odana Cafe, nr. Rly. Stn.	....	....	0937	....	....	....

Mondays to Fridays only

Service No.	540 ⊕	540 †	540 WF	541	540 ⊕	540
WINDERMERE, Main Rd., opp. Rly. Stn.dep	....	....	....	1645	....	....
Baddeley Clock........................ ,,	....	....	....	1648	....	....
Bowness, Kendal Bank Rd. corner .... ,,	....	....	....	1652	....	....
BOWLAND BRIDGE, Post Office........ ,,	0741	....	....	....	1658	....
Crosthwaite, Post Office .... ,,	0748	0802	1350	....	1705	1820
Underbarrow, Punch Bowl .... ,,	0755	0809	1357	....	1712	1827
Crook, Sun Inn........................ ,,	0806	0820	1408	....	....	....
Crook, Wild Boar Inn .... ,,	0813	....	....	1700	*	*
Crook, Sun Inn........................ ,,	0820	0820	1408	1707	....	....
KENDAL, Bus Stn., Blackhall Road ....arr	0833	0833	1421	1722	1728	1843

NO SERVICE ON SATURDAYS, SUNDAYS OR BANK HOLIDAYS.

CODE

WF—Weds., Fris. only.   †—Operates during School holidays.   *—Operates via Scout Scar.

⊕—School service—liable to suspension if not so required.

Timetable A for the Ribble 540 Kendal to Bowland Bridge service which, despite carrying no-one in 1976, was still running in 1978. Note how these services are almost entirely dependent on school runs.

no doubt be raised at this but all I'll say is if I had not taken them on board I would not have been able to live with myself.

And then I was sent to The Mighty Ribble, the Lake District no less. A quite scary amount of the red lines on our route map were school buses only, very few of these provided any 'real' service. Were it not for them, many of these routes would not have existed. We noticed that one, the 540 to the delightful village of Bowland Bridge, was carrying no-one, the local kids having grown up. As Cumbria County picked up the tab we felt obliged to tell them. Oh no, they said, keep it on, we must protect the network. It was this kind of blinkered thinking that almost brought the industry to its knees, saved in the nick of time by deregulation. Those who support regulation should dwell on what it was really like.

One day, I was looking after Grange over Sands depot and when I arrived I was told a driver had called in sick. The travel sales staff had 'pushed up', that is moved drivers to the shift in front, but had now run out and were left with no-one and a shift to cover. This was the Cartmel Schools Flookborough baths contract so there was nothing for it but to collect 'red setter' Leopard 53-seater no.492 and head off through the narrow lanes myself. The deal was that I took the first load plus teachers to the baths then shuttled back and forth taking different classes to and from the pool finally returning the teachers with the last lot. Whilst in bright spirits heading for Flookborough, I noticed the kids were less cheerful returning and enquiry revealed such things as 'we've got maths next'. The penultimate load was even more downcast and boarding asked 'please go slow driver, we've double Religious Instruction'. I dawdled through the lanes, took a long route, it was a delightful day, and my very late indeed arrival was greeted with smiles all round and copious amounts of Polo mints.

At Maidstone & District I was a bit of a hero at Borough Green depot by securing its first new bus since 1964 in the shape of 1978 Bristol VRT no.5846. On its first day, part of its duty was Meopham schools and it returned with three vandalised seats. We took it to the school next day and the very co-operative headteacher got all the kids back on it sitting where they had before thus exposing the villains. He took it up with their parents, two of which said that action would be taken at home. The third angrily asserted that their little darling would never do such a thing.

By now I was into high finance and, after a reorganisation in 1983 became responsible for all M&D's scholars season tickets. As they were worth over £2 million a year, it was of some note. The client was Kent County and relationships were bad, indeed my first meeting was truly dire and very unpleasant. The only saving grace was that the Kent guy had pictures of the Lake District on his office wall. A few days later, taking a pint of excellent Shepherd Neame beer in a lovely little pub, the Brown Jug at Upchurch (it was still there last time I looked), said Kent guy popped in, had a swift half and left without spotting me. I mentioned this to a chum at Kent who explained this guy was a great Sheps fan and was trying to visit all their pubs. They had just taken over a pub near my office so I rang and asked if we could have a chat about the system, I'd value his advice, and perhaps we could have a pint afterwards in this newly-acquired pub. We spent a happy time talking about the Lakes and enjoying Family Neame's finest and parted promising to chat about any concerns we had. There were no more problems we couldn't solve and the system worked well for both sides and, most importantly, the schoolkids.

One day I was contacted by the head of a school just along from my Chatham office. He explained the local paper was running a contest for schools to picture their paper being read in the most unusual of places and could I fix it for him to do so on the roof of one of our double-decks. In a moment of mental aberration I suggested joining him to apparently serve him champagne. The day duly arrived and he and I bedecked in formal clothing climbed with a table onto the roof of Olympian no.5902. It was chucking it down with rain and we gained access via an open-top DMS used for cleaning the lights in the Pentagon bus station (don't ask). The fitters moved the DMS away leaving us high and wet and I'll never forget the looks on their faces.

At one point we did a run for a school that, simply, didn't work. Bus companies tend to be very flexible with their schedules but there is a limit and we'd reached it with this one. There was no extra bus possible and with then, as now, no real will on behalf of the local authority to give priority to buses; it was all a bit of a disaster. A major duty change was needed to fix it. Every day one week the head rang me to say the bus was late and every time I explained our problem in detail. By Friday there was nothing I could add and when my secretary announced he was on the phone, I bottled it and asked her to say I'd gone out. (I was about to but, well, there it is, guilty as charged). A few minutes later she came into my office with that look secretaries, the true power in any organisation, reserve for those reputed to be senior to them. 'He just rang to say it was on time today.'

Prior to Bristol VRT no.5846's appearance, Maidstone & District Borough Green depot's frontline vehicles on trunk services like the 9 from Maidstone were 1964 Northern Counties Fleetlines. Delightful, reliable buses, they were getting past their prime by the time no.6084 is seen at Sevenoaks bus station in August 1977. Still a while before the advent of new VRTs, it's in company with one of the staggering number of 41-seat Leyland Nationals London Country seemed to find a use for, SNB263.

In the genes?

Mike Eyre

Transport author and historian, on the buses that took him to Manchester Grammar School

School didn't start my interest in buses – my folks reckoned it was in the genes. A great uncle was a designer of trams and bus bodies at Brush, Loughborough, and an uncle was involved in coach insurance and on the Manchester Transport Committee.

I was born in Moston, Manchester, on a development on which building was stopped by the war, with some houses half-finished; Moston Fields primary school was a couple of hundred yards walk. The war brought trolleybuses to Moston and even at primary school I could tell the difference between a Crossley and a Leyland.

In 1949 I passed the entrance exam for Manchester Grammar School. Known to this day as 'MGS', it has educated hundreds of famous people – and somehow it

managed to educate me. At MGS I found a master and half a dozen boys who were bus enthusiasts, which caused my interest in buses to (hopefully) become more intelligent, although never to the extent of tempting me into the industry. I spent my working life in computers and my only bus job was with Ribble at Manchester garage during summer university vacations.

The journey to MGS involved a cross-city trip – trolleybus to town, a walk from

Met Cam/Crossley-bodied Leyland no.1027 at the inwards stop across the road from Moston Fields School in 1955. The late 1930s housing started hereabouts and the stop had been the outer terminus of the 24 tram, hence the shelter. It was the closest stop to Mike's home but he usually walked to the Ben Brierley, where the 212x trolleybus terminated, giving him a choice of the 211, 212 or 212x. The second picture is at the Ben Brierley with English Electric-bodied Leyland no.1109 outbound; just visible in the right background is a 212x in the terminal loop.
Ray Dunning, C. Carter

Next stop MGS for 8ft-wide Leyland PD1 no.3150, outbound on the 40 in 1954. Similar no.3141 is inbound. Both pictures are at the junction of Dickenson Road (53 service) and Birchfields Road.
Ray Dunning

(Northenden), Leyland TS8s on the 31 (Bramhall), DD42s, TD5s and PD1s on the 41/42 (Chorlton and Didsbury) and North Western's lowbridge Leyland PD2s on the 64 to the airport at Ringway.

There were 1,400 boys at MGS. Just across Wilmslow Road was its female equivalent – Manchester High School for Girls (MHSG); half a mile or further out was the equally good Withington High School for Girls. The three schools' leaving times were staggered – allegedly to avoid overcrowding the Wilmslow Road buses. North Western's solution to this potential traffic problem was simple – they didn't bother to stop.

MGS was a day-school (no boarding) and folk came a long way – one in our form travelled from Southport every day – but in 1949 and 1950, when there was no such thing as the 'car school run', the corporation's MGS school buses were few and far between. Mornings were no problem – lots of buses on both roads going back on service to their garages. Evenings were different. A CVG5 on the 50x outwards to Sale, a TS8 single-decker on the 31x to Bramhall, two or three 8ft PD1s or DD42s on the 40x into Manchester and that was it: 263 seats for 1,400 kids.

Then something changed. The conversion of Birchfields Road garage from trams to buses was completed in 1950/1 and it was filled with Crossleys. Dozens of buses

High Street to Princess Street to catch bus 40 to MGS, which was and still is in Old Hall Lane, Rusholme, its large grounds more or less stretching from Birchfields Road to Wilmslow Road.

The 40 went along Birchfields Road. Just beyond Old Hall Lane it passed the modern bus garage and thence went to East Didsbury where it terminated outside Parrs Wood garage, which worked it with Leyland TD5s and Crossley DD42s, the latter soon replaced by 8ft-wide Leyland PD1s. We used the 40 because it was a long walk to Wilmslow Road although it had more buses – the awful turbo-transmitter Crossley DD42/3Ts on the 1 to Gatley, Daimler CVG5s on the 50

Leyland PD2s came to the 40 in 1954 and 1955. This is Northern Counties-bodied no.3324 outbound in Upper Brook Street in 1955. *Ray Dunning*

from it and Parrs Wood worked inwards to the city along Birchfields Road for the evening rush hour – but I doubt many would have stopped for MGS kids had not the son of Manchester's general manager, Albert Neal, started at MGS that year.

Suddenly more or less every bus from both garages going along Birchfields Road into town for the evening rush became an MGS school special. There was a line of a dozen 40x waiting at the Birch Hall Lane stop on Birchfields Road, often with an inspector to control them, and as one bus left another one joined the line. There were so many that we never had to stand up for the journey to town. If a bus looked like being full (or in my case if I wanted a trip on a PD2, TD5 or a Crossley Mancunian instead of a wheezing DD42 or ponderous PD1) you got on the next one … or the next … or the next …

I grew to hate travelling on the elderly, decaying Moston trolleybuses, with their leaking windows and roofs, floors awash with rainwater and missing seats, caused (as I now know) by indecision over their future and then by delay in delivery of the new BUTs. In 1955 trolleybuses went and for my last years at MGS, Moston had cross-city services

Two old Mancunians. Nos.2718 and (as yet unrenumbered) 723 in the yard at Parrs Wood in 1949, taken from the pavement on Kingsway. Both have come off rush-hour workings on the 40 service. *N. R. Knight*

worked by PD2s and CVG6s. That was fun. My parents, with the prospect of finally being rid of me, moved to Disley in posh Cheshire.

Twenty-three years later Eve and I also lived in Cheshire (in Marple Bridge) and our son, Richard, went to MGS. His school journey involved a train to Ashbury's and then a 53 bus to Birchfields Road. Not over-interested in transport, he was unimpressed by the attractions of a journey on the old Great Central line, passing the former Crossley Motors works, the works of Crossley Brothers, what was left of Gorton Tank, Beyer Peacock and so on, or the bus-a-minute 53 service. What he did notice was that every day a GMT Standard Atlantean left Marple Bridge on school service 712 to Manchester High School for Girls, its destination not more than 300 yards from MGS but restricted to carrying the young ladies of MHSG. A couple of phone calls to my friends in GMT got the restriction revised to include MGS boys. Something that Richard and his mates doubly appreciated.

Old Boys of MGS are known as 'Old Mancunians'; so are old Crossleys. I'll end with a picture of a couple of old Mancunians – you can find the real ones on *www.mgs.org.*

School buses from both sides

Malcolm Flynn

Bus enthusiast and photographer, recalls school buses as a pupil and as a teacher

I was brought up in Ruislip Gardens at the western end of the Central Line in Middlesex. We did not have a car then, so we relied on public transport – except Dad, who had his moped. Failing the eleven-plus, I started my secondary school in September 1961. I went to Queensmead School in South Ruislip and I travelled on the tube. Well, it was the easiest way! But, there was a good ten-minute walk at the other end, and that is where the bus came in. The 158 operated between Ruislip Lido and Watford

A Bowen's Leyland Leopard/ Plaxton at Bridgnorth in 1978 with children about to board for their return trip to Birmingham.
Malcolm Flynn

One double-deck coach is a lot cheaper than two single-deckers. Stevensons' Bristol VRT/ECW no.50 loads up with children from City Road Primary School, Birmingham, at the coach park in Chester in 1984. *Malcolm Flynn*

Junction and although it was only one stop from South Ruislip to school it was worth catching the bus, especially if it was raining. As a change from the tube, I would walk through to the Torcross Road stop and travel two fare stages to school. There were no school buses as such in this part of London.

Buses in my part of London were RTs, although RTWs had been used on the 158 for a few months in 1950, shortly before I was born. A revolution to hit the RT in the 1960s was the fitting of saloon heaters. It caused a sensation among my friends and we would congregate at Torcross Road stop waiting for RT738 to appear. It stood out from all the other RTs on the route, being in ex-works condition and with a heater.

I used the bus more from 1964 when, at 14, I had to pay full fare on the Tube. In those days it was possible to get a 'half-pass', which allowed the holder to travel on buses at the child rate for school purposes. I remember one occasion where I used my pass to get to Harrow Weald, became 13 to travel on a BR excursion to Chester on the newly electrified West Coast Main Line and then 18 for a pint in a Chester pub!

In 1966 the 158 was withdrawn between Harrow and Ruislip, being diverted to Rayners Lane. The 114 was diverted from Rayners Lane to Ruislip (extended to the Lido on Sundays) but remained RT-operated. Its conversion to AEC Swifts occurred after I left school.

When asked to send someone to talk about the pioneering Tracline 65 guided busway in suburban Birmingham, West Midlands PTE sent an MCW Metrobus and took the class to see it and sample it. *Malcolm Flynn*

There were occasions when we would travel on a dedicated 'school' bus – well, coach. There was the weekly swimming bus in the first year, either on a Duple-bodied Bedford SB or Ford Thames Trader (so I realised later).

Then there was the school trip. Towards the end of my time at Queensmead, I got on well with the second master and would be invited to go on visits to local industries. One particular visit was to the British Aircraft Corporation at Weybridge where we were supposed to visit various areas of the plant using the coach. Sadly this did not happen. Just after leaving the school, the driver discovered he could not engage second or third gear. We lurched to the site with the driver revving up in first and slamming the gear stick into fourth. The afternoon was spent in the Barnes Wallace Centre whilst mechanics replaced the gearbox! Priory Coaches of Uxbridge was the operator, I think.

My association with schools and buses continued after college when I started teaching. The swimming bus now was a Birmingham Standard provided by Lea Hall garage and later a Daimler Fleetline. Once established, I took over ordering coaches for school visits. With the daughter of L. F. Bowen working as a 'needlework' lady at my first school, Bowens Coaches was an obvious choice. It was from her that I learnt that Flights Coaches had been acquired. On another occasion, we ordered coaches from Midland Red, two LC7 Duple-bodied Leyland Leopards being supplied. Before leaving Birmingham, we had hired a Stevenson's Bristol VR to go to Chester, visited the guided busway on 'Tracline 65' service and West Midlands' Perry Barr garage where the children 'drove' a Daimler Fleetline (no nanny Health & Safety Executive then!); I had a go on my own, my first, on the school track.

Seen in the car park at Burton End School, Haverhill in 1992 is Hedingham Bristol VRT/ECW no.L194. This bus had come from Brighton Hove & District and was supplied at Malcolm's request. *Malcolm Flynn*

Moving to Suffolk in 1988 my involvement in ordering transport for school visits continued. Burton's Coaches of Haverhill was the operator of choice, usually Bedford YRTs or YMTs although DAFs featured towards the end of my teaching career. Part of the National Curriculum involved studying 'transport' and the opportunity was taken to hire double-deckers from Hedingham Omnibuses. A request for the Leyland-engined ex-Southdown Bristol VR was granted; on another occasion we visited the depot at Sudbury where the children were allowed to look round the buses and coaches. We used Hedingham to

Arriving back at Burton End School in 1995, Hedingham no.L1903, a Plaxton-bodied Leyland Tiger. *Malcolm Flynn*

Children mill around Hedingham Leyland Olympian/Alexander no.L160 at West Stow Country Park in 1993. *Malcolm Flynn*

provide transport from a Youth Hostel at Brandon. Michael, the driver, knew of my interest in buses and picked us up in a Leyland Lynx rather than a coach! L103, the Plaxton bus-bodied Leyland Leopard was not allowed – no tachograph. Cost was the overriding constraint in all hires.

The London RT played a small part in my journeys to school, but there had to be more to buses than just RTs and possibly RMs. Holidays to the south coast introduced me to the wonders of buses outside London and kindled my interest – Southdown's glorious Queen Marys and Maidstone &

District's revolutionary Leyland Atlanteans really caught my imagination. When London Transport announced an order for Atlanteans, I would regularly travel to Chalk Farm Depot on a Red Rover to try to see them. When I eventually found them, I was disappointed – M&D's were much more distinguished. My interest in buses took off when I discovered *Buses Illustrated* in 1964 and then met fellow enthusiasts at college. Alas, my attempts to interest my sons came to naught. At the age of four they could identify Daimler Fleetlines, Volvo-Ailsas and MCW Metrobuses – but that is as far as I got!

Novice conductor

James Freeman

Tells how conducting buses in Hampshire led to a career in senior transport

I joined Hants & Dorset in Winchester as a bus conductor in September 1974. I was 18 and fresh from my A-Levels, so it was a strange experience to find myself in the

Conductor Training School at West Marlands bus station opposite the Civic Centre in Southampton. We were under the watchful eye of Inspector Willoughby, a delightful man with a staccato delivery and a twinkle in his eye … He had the whole class of budding conductors issuing tickets to each other and writing up our waybills until they were coming out of our ears.

The experience was cut short for me – a phone call from Winchester depot called me back before I had 'graduated'. Mr Marsh, the operating superintendent, a huge and forbidding man with a bald head and glasses, told me that I knew enough anyway (he knew that I had been very interested in King Alfred Motor Services before it had closed the previous year and had covered a lot of the ground before I started) and I was needed to cover a school run that very afternoon!

Not only that, but it wasn't to be on the Hants & Dorset side of the business, for which I had been recruited, but the ex-King Alfred part. Although some 18 months had passed since the dreadful 28 April 1973, when King Alfred itself closed, the 'K-garage' as it was now known, still functioned largely as a business within a business.

So it was that at about 3.40pm we set out from the bus station – a former KA driver at the wheel (Pete Trott, a man I knew quite

well) and me on the back of AEC Bridgemaster WCG 107 (aka 2202) but still green and cream, rather than NBC poppy red. To be honest, I was more than a little nervous, for my baptism was to be by the little terrors of the 'Top School' – the Montgomery of Alamein School in Romsey Road.

ABOVE: WGC 106, sister to AEC/Park Royal Bridgemaster WGC 107 on 29 November 1975 on a farewell tour organised by James to mark the demise of the last bus in King Alfred livery with Hants & Dorset; this was more than 18 months after the takeover. It is going under the bridge of the closed Watercress Line between Winchester and Alresford at Springvale.

LEFT: On the same occasion, WGC 106 on route 17 in Highcliffe (Winchester), showing the King Alfred blinds that were put back in the bus for the tour.

By Bus to School

My nerves were fully justified, for as we swung into the parking area there was just time to dive off the back of the bus as seemingly hundreds of screaming kids swarmed on board. I judged it best to leave them to it, so walked round to Pete at the front to confer. After a few minutes, the bus started to rock alarmingly from side to side as the boys upstairs ran from first one side to the other. They knew the characteristics of the Bridgemaster, with its air suspension – so I had to go back on board and tell them to stop it! Amazingly, they did.

Come five minutes past four off we went. I had to get round the bus and collect 4p from each child (or clip their weekly tickets in the right place). The bus was full, so there were almost 80 of them, and I had ten minutes at most to 'get 'em in'. As I later found, some of our drivers were less than sympathetic to their conductor's plight in this respect and would put their foot down, but Pete took pity on me and drove slowly.

I was determined that these little monsters wouldn't get the better of me! 'Who are you, Mister?' someone shouted. 'You're new, in't you?', said another. I just kept going, issuing the tickets and collecting the money. As I watched, I saw a weekly ticket pass under a seat – so I caught that one! Meanwhile, the boys at the front upstairs had opened up the blind box (Hants & Dorset had fitted three-track numerals and moved the handles from the cab to the front of the lower saloon) and were merrily winding the numbers round to the evident confusion of waiting passengers!

Still, before too long I was saying goodbye to the last child and we were heading back to the Broadway for our next trip – something more ordinary with grown-up passengers.

I arrived back in the bus station, tired but pleased with myself for surviving this first ordeal by youth! 'How did you get on?', asked one of my new-found colleagues. 'Oh, fine!', said I. Well, it was almost true!

So started my career as a bus conductor. It lasted six months before I went on to Bristol to be a junior clerk. The hours were long but running up and down the stairs kept me fit and I earned lots of money quite quickly. Best of all, I laid the foundations for a career in the bus industry which I am still enjoying today.

An enthusiast's tale

David Harvey

Transport writer and historian, recalls his Birmingham childhood

There has been a theory, around for many years, which suggests that bus enthusiasts, historians and preservationists are about the same age as either the vehicles they own or their period of interest. This would explain why, at the first HCVC bus rally in 1958 nearly all of the buses which were entered dated from before World War II and a few even dated from the end of the 1920s. Interestingly, many of the owners were themselves of prewar construction, including preservation pioneers such as the late Prince J. Marshall (1937-1979), thus probably proving the theory.

So where did I get my enthusiasm for buses? I first saw the light of day in Heathfield Road Maternity Hospital, Birmingham in January 1948 to a father and mother who had little interest in transport other than catching a bus or a tram when required. My grandfather, who retired during my first year, must have taken me for pushchair rides on to the nearby Kingstanding Road and to the more distant Perry Barr which was the terminus of the no.6 tram. I cannot now lay claim to remembering the trams on this route as I was three weeks short of my second birthday when this service was abandoned but there is a vague memory … of open-balcony trams and getting off in my grandad's arms and being held, terrifyingly loosely, over the parapet of Perry Barr station's railway bridge. Years later there was also a series of vivid dreams of travelling, presumably in a pushchair pushed by my granddad, along a lane without a footpath with a high fence on the right-hand side and distant corrugated iron gable-ended buildings beyond the fence. Peeking above the top of the tall fence were the top decks of corporation buses which tantalisingly could not be identified. Twenty-five years later I felt the colour drain from my face when standing at a sales stand; I had found a photograph taken inside the fence of over 50 withdrawn prewar and wartime Birmingham buses awaiting sale on the Holford Drive dump in Perry Barr.

This was one of the 17 Metro-Cammell-bodied Daimler CVD6 that were delivered to Perry Barr garage when new in the autumn of 1951. It is standing alongside the impressive bus shelters in Kingstanding Road at the junction with Hawthorn Road behind the bus. These were the buses that David's dad chose to draw, which was a little disappointing as David preferred buses with polished exposed radiators. The one advantage that these buses had as far as a three year old boy was concerned was that for the first time with a Birmingham bus, the saloon window overlooking the bonnet had a curved bottom profile that enabled him to stand up and just see over the bonnet to the road ahead.
C. W. Routh

One of the 15 somewhat idiosyncratically-styled AEC Regent 0961 RTs pulls away from the bus stop outside Yardley Grammar School in about the same year as David started his secondary education there in 1959. It is travelling towards the City Centre on the 44A route. Through the distant trees behind the bus is the entrance to Tyseley engine shed whose juxtaposition to the school began David's long-term interest in steam locomotives as, providing they were wearing their egg, green and black school ties, David and his mates could 'bunk the shed' once a week with just a nod to the foreman on duty. *F. W. York*

So Grandfather Harry, whose hand I tightly held on to when we went to Ashted on a no.10 tram to collect corn for the chickens he kept in the back garden and who also took me for a ride to Yardley and back on a pair of six-wheel trolleybuses, started off my interest in buses and thankfully showed me Birmingham tramcars, admittedly as a young child, before they finally were consigned to the scrapyard in July 1953.

My dad was a good artist, particularly ink caricatures of friends and work colleagues and of rather delicate watercolours usually of watery lakeland landscapes and hills covered with forests. Buses were definitely not in his painting scene, but coupled with my grandfather's excursions and my infant pestering, dad was badgered into doing about three or four watercolour paintings of buses coming down Kingstanding Road's steep hill opposite the Greenholm public house. The previous year I'd vaguely remembered seeing buses with black radiators, starting handles and square-looking bodies travelling towards Perry Barr. These were the last of the wartime rebodied petrol-engined AEC Regents, but had disappeared before dad went out to draw some of the newest buses, which were part of

Birmingham City Transport had 170 exposed-radiator all-Crossley DD42/6s which were delivered between the autumn of 1949 and the early summer of 1950. No.2324 entered service on New Year's Day 1950 and was the longest survivor of the Acocks Green Crossleys, being withdrawn on 31 March 1967. It is seen in Deritend when operating on the 44 route which was the shortest of the variations working along Warwick Road. *R. H. G. Simpson*

Perry Barr garage's small allocation of the 1951 Daimler CVD6s working on the 33 route to Kingstanding. It was also at the same spot when our next-door neighbour, who was a bus driver and instructor, was killed by a former colleague who swerved his lorry towards his bus to frighten him as a 'joke' as he stood in the dual carriageway having just got out of the cab of the bus. I think it was the first time I saw a hearse carrying a coffin of someone I'd known. Looking back, the paintings were quite good, but to me as a three-year-old, they were brilliant: my dad had done them! They were safely stored by my mum for over 45 years but after her death they disappeared and with them went a glimpse of my infant enthusiasm.

My mum's brother had left Scotland during the war to work in a reserved occupation at the Harland & Wolff shipyard in Belfast and subsequently married and settled down in the city. My aunt and uncle also lived coincidentally near to the 33 route operated by Belfast Corporation, but this was altogether a different kettle of fish. These were big six-wheeled red-and-white painted trolleybuses going to and from the nearby Carr's Glen terminus across the city to Cregagh as a southbound 33 and a 35 northbound. So 33 became my favourite number as we lived near to Birmingham's 33 route and so did my relatives in Belfast.

Wind on a few years and my parents had left the 33 route to live in Greet on the 44A bus route. The last buses to operate in Birmingham with wheel discs, so common on Birmingham's 'new-look' front buses from 1950 until about 1955 when one reputedly came off and

chariot-like sliced off a woman's leg, were the 15 Park Royal-bodied AEC Regent III 0961 RT-types numbered 1631-1645. These buses were almost exclusively operated by Acocks Green garage and managed to keep their rear wheel discs until about 1957 or 1958. They were splendid buses but had a unique four-bay body with shades of London Transport and Park Royal design but with Birmingham's specifications superimposed on to and inside the body. They had angled staircases and at the front of both saloons the woodwork was painted white with hardly any of the usual varnished wood that so characterised Birmingham's buses of the time. There came a time when every one of the 15 was different

Overlooked by the Divis Mountain, Belfast's Carr's Glen trolleybus terminus in Ballysillan Road was at a turning circle at the junction with Joanmount Gardens and was only one stop beyond where David's aunt and uncle lived. Leaving the terminus on the cross-city 33 service to Cregagh is AEC 664T trolleybus no.64 with a Harkness body. These were impressive six-wheelers which had blue leather seating and a wonderful smell of electricity reminding David of his Trix Twin model railway locomotives which after several hours of play had a similar aroma. The trolleybus is overtaking bus no.366, one of the 98 Harkness-bodied Daimler CVG6s built between 1952 and 1954. *R. F. Mack*

Preserved no.2489, 'Christine the Crossley', stands at Burton-on-Trent Town Hall in June 2008 when operating on a specially-routed town service. The bus is now almost back to its as-built condition with the only incorrect detail being the tiny 1953 Coronation flag holder located beneath the destination blind. So here is Birmingham's sole surviving Crossley, which has probably the earliest surviving New Look front in existence. It is a rare beast and one that, despite its sturdy construction, is a Crossley that works properly. Dating from 1950, the bus has less body sag than its owner who is just two years older! *D. R. Harvey*

with some major mechanical or bodywork modification and before I took my eleven-plus examination I could tell one from another at a distance of … well before you could see the registration. Acocks Green's exposed radiator Crossley-bodied Crossley DD42/6s were also interesting buses as in the hands of a driver well-versed in the art of using a clutch and gearbox they were a more interesting ride than the 'new-look' front Metro-Cammell-bodied Guy Arab III Specials that were also allocated to the same garage. The Crossleys were quieter, gave a very comfortable ride and despite their reputation elsewhere in the country for being short on power, were surprisingly speedy. The father of one of my classmates could testify to this as he was caught speeding on Stratford Road by the police doing 46mph – and in gear!

The passing of the examination enabled me to go to Yardley Grammar School in Warwick Road, Tyseley on 3 September 1959 – the day war broke out 20 years earlier. My interest in buses was such that by the spring of 1959 I had spotted every Birmingham bus in service as well as later interesting demonstrators which were always allocated to Lea Hall garage on the other side of the City.

The Ian Allan ABC was wonderful and so I started spotting again only this time taking the chassis numbers from licence discs in the cab, chassis number plates in the cabs, from dumb irons or, in the case of Crossleys, on the nearside front of the chassis visible only by peering under the nearside wheelarch and upwards just in front of the front tyre.

By the time I'd completed this strange spotting task most of the 1947-9 stock of Daimler CVA6s and CVD6s had gone and I had ceased to call myself a 'bus spotter', but a 'bus enthusiast' as a group of us, all fourth form Yardleians had formed the Yardley Grammar School Bus and Railway Enthusiasts Society. This was achieved with the help of our music master, David Richmond, who had become a hallowed hero as he'd had two photographs published in *Buses Illustrated* magazine. This embryonic interest in details eventually manifested itself in my long-time membership of the Birmingham Transport Historical Group, my first attempts to write books and articles, and to collect photographs especially of Birmingham trams, trolleybuses and buses – please, has anyone a photograph of either 2652 (JOJ 652) or 2757 (JOJ 757)? Why 'Railway'? Well, opposite Yardley Grammar School was

Tyseley locomotive power depot, better known as 84E, with an allocation of ex-Great Western Railway 'Halls', 'Granges', 2-8-0s, 'Prairie Tanks' as well as various types of 0-6-0PT and a few Great Western Railcars. I didn't stand a chance, much in the same way that a few years later when I played rugby for the school, my college and several local teams up to an almost serious level, while studying geography to postgraduate level, real ale, the tipple of rugby players and geographers, was always well appreciated and I had a foot in both camps!

That is almost the end of the story, except that three years after having qualified as a geography teacher I joined the 2489 Group, which had been formed in August 1969 to preserve the 'new-look' front Birmingham Crossley no.2489 (JOJ 489). I took my PSV test in 1977 and today the bus, repainted as many times as the Forth Bridge and with numerous engine rebuilds to overcome the frailties of the oil-leak inducing Crossley engine, looks as good as it did when it first entered service in July 1950. No.2489 is known by my family and group members as 'Christine the Crossley', a name given to the bus by my daughter when she was about four years old.

So back to the beginning. There has been a theory, around for many years, which suggests that bus enthusiasts, historians and preservationists are about the same age as either the vehicles they own or their period of interest. Born in 1948, with a 1950 bus and writing about local history and transport in the first 80 years of the 20th century. Case proved I think!

Happy days!

Peter Hesketh

Transport enthusiast and author, looks back at a Lancashire childhood

The word 'surreal' was not in my vocabulary as a seven year old in 1954. If it had been, that is how I might have described the Ribble Alexander rebodied Leyland Titan TD, as it became more and more enveloped in the snowstorm, its back-end resting in the field in Potter Lane, Samlesbury, its front-end protruding through the hedge, wheels off the ground, pointing skywards, abandoned, all in darkness, but with the windscreen wiper going back and forth, losing the battle against the blizzard.

Peter on his bike, setting off to Preston Grammar School when in the first form, ready to bus-spot on the way.

My first year at school had been at St Matthews on New Hall Lane in Preston, among the soot descending into the cramped playground from the terraced houses looming menacingly around it, the winter smog and the varied selection of childhood diseases that eventually were the deciding factors to move me to the 60-pupil village school on the road out to Blackburn. So, I escaped daily to a rural idyll where only the surrounding countryside and the banks of the River Ribble threatened, to a sound education based sometimes on harsh discipline, but enjoying every minute of it, not least my daily journeys from my home and back; by bus, of course (and as an unaccompanied six year old).

Incredibly in those days and at that time of the morning there were three buses together for me to choose from at the Cemetery bus stop. The weekday headway on the 'New Road' service to Blackburn and beyond to Burnley or Rochdale was 20 minutes. The morning pattern was always the same: a Ribble and a Scout double-decker and a Ribble single-decker, but in any order – a wonderful state of affairs for a bus-mad schoolboy who'd been so afflicted for as long as he can remember. The standard fare tended to be all-Leyland lowbridge PD2s and a Royal Tiger, again with Leyland bodywork. Before the advent of Ribble and Scout's PD3s and highbridge-working the newest double-deckers were their standards and I thought they were brand-new, as on a return journey I relished the smell of new paint on one of Ribble's, not realising that the 1951 bus had just been repainted. Adding to the fascination was the unusual, such as the single-decker appearing along New Hall Lane as one of the Burlingham-bodied PS1 Tigers or a rebodied prewar Titan, hence the excitement in the snow.

The double-decker had been first, but was full, and I can't remember what came next. In any event as it struggled through the fast-falling snow out into the countryside I saw a crowd standing at my stop just past the junction with Potter Lane, down which I had to walk the quarter of a mile to school. The crowd was the complement of the first bus, which, on pulling away from the stop having dropped off a couple of other Preston pupils, had not been able to gain traction up the hill in the snow and, even worse, had started to slide backwards, its driver obviously attempting to stop it by putting a left-hand lock on, but the steepness of the lane pulled the bus into it and the hedge!

Wow! I couldn't wait until dad came home from work to relate the tale, simple things keeping the young bus-spotter happy. Like the time when work was well under way on the county's first motorway, the Preston Bypass, which was half a mile from school. The building of the bridge over the River Ribble meant that the A59 road was diverted temporarily up on to the new carriageway and down it. Being ever-enthralled by buses in unusual places, one everlasting memory is being on the middle bus, trailing some distance behind the first, a PS1, as it bounced over the hill, through toiling Euclid dump trucks (just like my Dinky model) and Sherman tanks (used to recover Euclid dump trucks).

Today's schoolchildren would be amazed at what was expected of us in the 1950s. Our

Preston Corporation no.65, a 1940 all-Leyland Titan TD7 with a chassis believed to have been a Leyland Motors TD6 prototype, was a particular favourite of Peter's, and he travelled on it to Preston Grammar School. Here it is waiting on Deepdale Road for pupils to swarm aboard on the afternoon special from the grammar school to town.
Mike Rhodes collection

Peter was less than impressed by Preston Corporation's ambitious rebuilding of 27ft-long lowbridge rear entrance all-Leyland Titan PD2s into 30ft-long highbridge forward entrance buses like this one, between 1959 and 1962, preferring the later highbridge buses that received the same treatment.
Ian Allan Library

headmistress lived in Preston and sometimes travelled with us. On the way home, before alighting, we were expected to approach her, doff our caps and wish her 'Good afternoon'. I curled up with embarrassment one day, when, having performed my deference, I made my way to the back of the bus, only to realise my escape was blocked; it was a new Leyland PD3, and I had to retrace my steps, past giggling pals and scowling headmistress (who had coined and used to cutting effect 'Stupid boy' long before Dad's Army) to the forward entrance.

In 1958, I moved to Preston Grammar School. The journey to there on Deepdale Road, a cock-stride from Preston Corporation's garage, presented options; walk or cycle along Blackpool Road to school, take a bus into town and then one on the inner circle, Fulwood via Deepdale (and pass the garage) or use a strange corporation service, the peaks and Sundays-only 'cross-town', as crews called it, Lane Ends to the Cemetery. With the mnemonic route letters, LE over C, it travelled along Blackpool Road, although

at the Lane Ends end it continued half a mile further on to the Ashton A's turning circle at Pedders Lane. Its description was something of a misnomer, as it was the only one not to actually cross town; all routes were then linked through the town centre. This was a final haunt of one of the last four prewar buses in the fleet, which were scrapped in 1959, all-Leyland TD7 no.65, its chassis thought to have started life as a TD6 test-bed for Leyland's MkIII engine and converted to a TD7 before bodying.

One morning, as usual, I was on the last minute and realised that I didn't have time to walk, cycle or go through town (my preferred route, to see more buses), so I legged it to the terminus on Blackpool road for the LE C, which had just spun around the Cemetery roundabout. This was a manoeuvre that had always fascinated me, being enthralled equally by termini. Running up towards the rear of the bus, to my delight, I realised it was no.65, identifiable by its upper deck emergency exit, similar but not identical to the postwar type but, I didn't realise, fitted to Leyland bodies from 1939.

In my years at the grammar school the Blackpool Road journey provided no end of bus-spotting experiences, as it crossed the routes to Moor Nook, Ribbleton and Holme Slack, besides the inner and outer circles at the far end of my part of it, and the Farringdon Park at the home end. Moor Nook was chosen as the first for the corporation's Leyland PD3s in 1958 and to sample them I came home one afternoon via town and then went out of my way on the MN. My mother accepted the reason for the lateness with her usual tutting and head-shaking but I was able to give my father a full debrief over the tea table about my sampling of the new buses. On top of all that, Blackpool Road was used by the corporation as a test route, highlights being lowbridge PD1 no.6's first venture out as the breakdown wagon and PD3 no.50, after conversion from a PD2, the first highbridge one to be treated, and I remember thinking that it looked super, something that couldn't be said about the lowbridge rebuilds.

Yes, for the young Peter Hesketh, school days were happy days!

Freedom and independence

Peter Huntley

Transport consultant-turned-manager, celebrates the freedom that school buses offered

My regular use of buses started with journeys to school in 1966 heading for West Hartlepool's Elwick Road School and later the Technical High School for Boys. This made me a regular user of the corporation's cross-town services 4 and 6, but also provided the introduction to a wider world of independent travel that was perhaps to shape my life and certainly my career.

I still strongly believe that being able to use public transport confidently gives young people an incredible gift of personal freedom

Traditional West Hartlepool fare when the young Peter Huntley first became aware of buses included Roe-bodied Daimler CVG6s like this 1953 example in Church Street. *G. Mead*

One of West Hartlepool's 1950 all-Leyland Titan PD2/3s. *Ian Allan Library*

previously cuffed around the ear for pressing a bell) and the bizarre notion of alighting from a centre exit – and with doors rather than an open platform to boot! Soon after 'British West Hartlepool' was to disappear forever in the amalgamation with Hartlepool and the merged operation was to enjoy the new-found freedom to buy its best-ever bus – the Bristol RE, acquiring no fewer than 58 of these fine machines over an eight-year period of transformation of the network and its operations.

Single-deck buses were still a novelty in 1966 for me, however, and I much preferred the extra capacity of the final two Leyland PD2s delivered the previous year which impressed the locals with their new Formica internal trim and fluorescent lights. With two decks of course came the benefit of a choice of smoke-filled upper deck and breathable lower deck seats. These fine machines (BEF 27/28C) proved to be Hartlepool's last double-decks, the last open platform buses and the last with conductors, and saw the watershed for buses as we knew them.

Even then I was passionate about trying to convert anyone who would listen to the benefits of bus travel and with a maximum child fare of 3d (just over 1p in 'new money')

and wish I could persuade more parents of today how important this independence could and should be to their children.

The year 1966 felt like it was one when 'all was happening' and my earliest memories of those journeys are of 1949 Daimlers and 1950 Leyland Titans starting to give way to the 'new-fangled' (and recently authorised) full-size one-person-operated single-deck buses. My first experience of the bright new future was the shock of PEF 19 (a Strachan-bodied Leyland Leopard) requiring the strange practice of paying the driver as you boarded, ringing a bell to get off (I was

Hartlepool Corporation moved from double-deckers to batches of Strachans-bodied Leyland Leopard L1s in 1964/5. *D. M. Stuttard*

ABOVE: Hartlepool famously went on to buy a substantial fleet of ECW-bodied Bristol RELL6L – its 'best-ever bus' in Peter's view. *Kevin Lane*

LEFT: Peter was shocked to find that buses in nearby Middlesbrough used letters instead of route numbers. This is a Daimler Fleetline/Northern Counties on route F. *G. Coxon*

I enjoyed exploring my home town, working out service inter-working to get a tour of the town for one fare. Imagine my shame, having convinced a group of friends to try this with me, to find we were on a duplicate that dropped out of service at the wrong end of town, leaving us spent-up and with a long walk home.

Hartlepool, like many other towns, had a distinct and different feel that was confirmed by its buses and the municipal colours, on everything from the bus to the lamp-posts and contrasts markedly with today's national brands and identities. School rugby games in Stockton, Middlesbrough and Darlington with their green, blue and white buses contrasting to our red ones, felt like journeys into foreign lands and crossing the 'frontier' of the Transporter Bridge into Middlesbrough I was shocked to find that their bus services had letters instead of numbers. Now how weird is that?

From Northern to Northern

Andy Izatt

Transport journalist, on schooldays in Sussex and a Scottish connection

I have a confession to make: my enthusiasm for buses was not inspired by travelling to school on them although I took a much keener interest when I did start.

My parents were brought up in the north-east of Scotland and both were students at Aberdeen University. My father was an electronics engineer and he moved south to Surrey with my mother, a teacher, in 1959 for his first job with the BBC. By that time my elder brother had been born although it would be another four years before I came along.

The family's association with the north-east of Scotland meant that that was where the annual summer holiday was taken for many years. Surviving grandparents lived in Stonehaven and it was not long before my brother and I started to take note of the vehicles of Alexander (Northern) painted as they were in that stunning yellow and cream livery that I still believe has been unmatched by any other operator.

As a proportion of its fleet, Northern had fewer double-deckers than virtually any other nationalised bus company. As we were invariably in Stonehaven during the school holidays, a sight of one of its magnificent Northern Counties- or Alexander-bodied Leyland Titans was a rare and treasured treat. Visits to Aberdeen were much anticipated as these fine vehicles ran to Culter and that also engendered an interest in the corporation buses. Purists will wring their hands in anguish, but I always thought the orange band added to Aberdeen's green and cream when Grampian Regional Transport was formed in 1974 was a great improvement.

ABOVE: Andy behind the wheel of LS7, the first of London Transport's big Leyland National order at Showbus in 1976, aged 13.

BELOW: Andy road tests a Reptons Coaches Van Hool T916 Astron for routeONE magazine in December 2008, aged 45.

Then there were the three Leyland Nationals – fine buses!

In 1973, when I was 10 my parents decided to send me to a small fee-paying school just outside Horsham in Sussex called

Andy had great affection for the Aldershot & District Dennis Loline IIIs with their sliding doors and single 'bus spotter' seats upstairs at the front nearside. This is one of the last survivors of the 1965 Weymann-bodied batch, seen in 1979 in Alder Valley days.
P. R. Nuttall

St John's College. We lived in the growing Surrey village of Cranleigh, around 12 miles north west of Horsham, so that meant I was going to travel to school by bus for the first time, on route 283, previously 33, which originated in Guildford.

That was the good news. The bad news was our local bus company was National Bus Company-owned Alder Valley, an amalgamation of Aldershot & District and Thames Valley – two companies with very different cultures. What a let-down! Now don't get me wrong. I had great affection for the Aldershot Dennis Loline IIIs with their sliding doors and single 'bus-spotter' seats upstairs at the front nearside that still ran through Cranleigh to Ewhurst on the 23, later 273, but we had no such luxuries on the 283. We had to suffer short-wheelbase, two-door Marshall-bodied Bristol REs, possibly the worst buses I have ever had the misfortune to travel on – and they were almost new! They were noisy, smelly and uncomfortable, and to this day it's a mystery to me why they had middle doors and steps that only seemed to

provide training for budding Olympic ski jumpers. The drivers hated those middle exits, not using them wherever possible, which just confused passengers, and it didn't seem long before they were invariably taped off with some ticket machine roll.

I remember a small party of Americans climbing aboard a Marshall RE with their suitcases one day. One made a polite comment through gritted teeth about how great it was that here in England we still had rural buses, but the culture shock was obvious and unforgettable. I think they felt they had just been given an insight as to what bus travel might be like in Colombia.

Just occasionally the schedulers took pity on us and we were treated to a real bus, an AEC Reliance. Alder Valley had several

Not a fan of the Alder Valley Bristol RELLs, Andy regarded them as marginally better than rare ECW-bodied Ford R1014s like this one.

'Fine buses' in Andy's eyes, one of Aberdeen Corporation's three Leyland Nationals in Union Street.
Gavin Booth

batches, some having been rebodied by Metro-Cammell in the 1960s, but they were always comfortable vehicles despite their age. Then one day we had our first Leyland National. Wow! Now I know the purists will have written me off as an ignorant heathen by this stage because I've had the audacity to be rude about a Bristol. There was worse – the ECW- and Plaxton-bodied Fords that Alder Valley ran – and I'm fully aware of the National's well-proven shortcomings, but for us long-suffering RE users these were spaceships from heaven.

I have made my living for some years now as a bus and coach trade journalist so I've had plenty of opportunities to be among the first to try new models – the first from the UK to ever set eyes on a Mercedes-Benz Citaro for example

– but I can think of no bus that has had the impact that first Leyland National had on my perceptions of bus travel. I know the critics will scoff, but I believe there was a tremendous amount that was right about the National from a passenger's perspective. These were easy access, comfortable, spacious, well-illuminated vehicles that rode well. Remember the blue fluorescent saloon lights? Compared to the RE, travelling on a National was akin to a first motorbus ride after putting up with a horse and cart.

As St John's College was outside Horsham it bought a Burlingham-bodied Ford Thames from Billingshurst Coaches in 1973 to transport us 'day boys' to and from the town centre. If I had a fiver for every time the 283 was late and we missed said coach

In the 'stunning' Alexander Northern yellow/cream colours, a Daimler Fleetline/ECW on the Culter-Dyce service in Aberdeen in 1980.

and had to walk to school I would be a rich man. Driven by a thoroughly likable chap called Bob – well it would be a Bob wouldn't it – the Thames lasted just four years. Death was sadly long and lingering. Today's youth are often criticised for their lack of respect of other people's property, but it wasn't a lot different in the 1970s – although there wasn't the jealousy and nastiness we see today. First to go were the seat cushions.

With the Thames's demise, local operator Mitchell Compact was contracted to cover the work. Jimmy Mitchell could lay claim to being one of the first independent bus operators in the Horsham area back in the 1920s, but what was left of the family business based in nearby Warnham had been sold to Stedman of Crawley trading as Compact Coaches in 1973.

I well remember Mitchell Compact's first day on our school run. A smart P-registered Duple Dominant Ford turned up and the headmaster strode aboard to take stock. He asked the driver if it would always be this vehicle. 'Well maybe,' was the mumbled response and sure enough as each day passed the vehicles got older, but this was a fascinating eight-strong fleet. There were two M-registered Duple Fords that taught me that the year of registration didn't always match the year built because the body plates on these coaches clearly indicated that they were two years older. Then there were three wonderful Bedford VALs that just seamed to glide along, one of those rebodied Alder Valley Reliances and – beyond all belief – an Alexander (Northern) AEC Monocoach from the 1950s.

I'll never forget the first day it turned up. I just couldn't believe my eyes! I ended up going to school on a Northern bus after all and thankfully this fine vehicle has been preserved in the north-east of Scotland.

Monarchs and Cavaliers

Clive King

Bus company manager, at school and on holiday in and around London

I grew up in South Norwood, London SE25 during the 1950s. My parents never owned a car. In the years after World War 2, the area was drab with smoke blackened buildings, bombsites and frequent periods of smog.

There were few motorcars and most were black, small, uncomfortable and would not start on winter mornings.

The true 'Monarch of the Road' was the bright red, double-deck London Transport bus. To me, it was spacious, comfortable, smooth-running and fast. Yes, fast! We lived near trolleybus route 654 and the trolleys would easily see off the likes of Austin 7s and Morris 8s. So, for that matter, would the RTs. I used to sit looking out across the rear platform watching them fall behind.

In London, primary schools were all walking distance from home. Consequently, I would pester my Mum to take me to the ends of the local routes to explore our surroundings from the front, upper deck seats. Caterham Valley, Oxford Circus, Raynes Park, Tufnell Park and Woolwich Free Ferry. Wonderful!

Sadly, the trolleys went in March, 1959, and, at first glance, the RTs all seemed the same. When I looked harder, I noticed the variations. Then, at Penge, I saw RFs.

In Croydon, some of the buses were green. At Bletchingley, an RLH looked ancient to me. Dorking yielded a GS – which I thought was a Thames. I was fascinated.

We had relatives in Thornton Heath, near the yard in Nursery Road used by Margo's Coaches. They had double-deckers 'straight out of the ark'. Locals called them 'workmen's buses'. They were really interesting and, with hindsight, were prewar provincial Regents and utilities.

Summer holidays were accessed by coach – usually Bourne & Balmer. We changed over in their Dingwall Road coach station in Croydon. The full-front monsters looked so modern and, when I stood close, so tall … and where was the engine?

Primary school did eventually yield bus and coach trips. We travelled weekly to Thornton Heath baths on HOY 237, which we thought was powered by an elastic band. It was a beautiful Leyland PS1/Strachan in dark green lined in gold.

In 1961, there was a special event in Croydon. We were collected by two Surrey Motors coaches. The first of them was ultra-modern. We had seen nothing like it – 'out of this world'. It was 700 RPA – my first sighting of the brilliant Harrington Cavalier.

I started at Selhurst Grammar School for Boys in September 1962. Travel to the Junior Department in Croydon was by RT on route 12. I was already intrigued by buses and coaches and one lunch time I saw another boy in my form, Paul Everett, clutching a book about buses: the inevitable Ian Allan ABC. We had a long chat, which led to a Red Rover – all the way to Barnet. From the top of the stairs, the upper deck of the pre-production batch RML seemed to extend forward a very long way – ultimately to a lifelong interest and career in transport.

Two Harrington-bodied AEC Reliances from the Surrey Motors fleet; in 1961 saw 700 RPA on the left, his first Cavalier body and it was 'out of this world', in Clive's words.

Gilletts and the Big Company

Philip Kirk

Bus company manager, is kept in order by a conductress in County Durham

My association with school buses started in 1973, when I first attended the local Grammar School in Wingate, County Durham, two villages away from home. The bus was essentially a duplicate to the Durham to Hartlepool service bus operated by Gillett Brothers of Quarrington Hill. As my father had worked for the company and was well known to the staff, any misbehaviour on my part was ruled out before it had ever begun.

The regular vehicle was an AEC Reliance with a Plaxton Highway body having coach seats in a bus shell. By this date, it was seven years old but it was always kept in immaculate condition; perhaps because for a long time the coaches in the Gilletts fleet were only 45–seaters and OPT 852D was therefore the nearest to a full coach for a party of 51. Strict order was kept by a regular conductress – Hettie – and woe betide anyone who so much as thought of stepping out of line. She must have demonstrated something of that attitude to Gilletts as she refused to use any of the 'new fangled'

Setright ticket machines, and so the company retained two Bellgraphic machines for her use.

The way in which Hettie collected the fares was interesting too. Standing by the door, Hettie would watch the children getting on and for each child she would record the fare in ballpoint pen on to the ticket then issue it. When everyone had got on at that stop, she would be left with a stream of tickets hanging from the machine and so then she moved up the bus, knowing that that number of children owed her their bus money!

Gilletts was purchased by United Automobile Services in late 1974 and a family move to 'bright lights, big city' Hartlepool meant that I was now travelling on a different section of the same route to reach school. I could therefore witness at first hand how the Big Company made a complete mess of its acquisition. This seemed to centre on changing the inherited fleet and replacing the immaculately kept AECs with coaches drafted in from elsewhere in the United fleet or

A late purchase by Gillett Bros, Quarrington Hill, was this 1972 AEC Reliance/Plaxton Highway, used here on the Bishop Auckland-Hartlepool service. The company sold to United Auto in 1974. *G. Coxon*

The new order at Quarrington Hill – a former Gillett 1972 AEC Reliance/Plaxton Highway in NBC red for United, left, and a similar, 1970 bus on the right still in Gillett livery but with United fleet number. *G. Coxon*

indeed from sister National Bus Company fleets. United had a batch of five Bristol LH touring coaches, fleet numbers 1081–5 (BHN 981–5H), and two or three of these were allocated to what had now become United service 20. With manual door controls, they were hardly well suited for bus operation, and I expect that it was thought that the conductor could do this. Except that at busy times, the conductor would be trapped down the saloon and because of the narrow coach gangway unable to fight past the standing passengers to get to the door. The conductors would nominate me to help, and I suppose therefore my first job in the bus industry was to take charge of the opening and closing of the doors on these coaches – there were less stringent Health and Safety rules in the 1970s!

By the time my school career had finished in 1978, I also knew the intricacies of door mechanisms on former Ribble coaches and ex–Crosville Bristols. All of this propelled me into a job as Junior Clerk at Hartlepool Borough Transport, which curiously started with potatoes. But that is for another time …

United drafted in various vehicles to run the former Gillett routes, including Bristol LH6L/Plaxton coaches with manual door control that were, says Philip, 'hardly well suited for bus operation'. Here is one of the LH6Ls doing what it was bought for – on an extended tour in Edinburgh in 1971. *G. R. Mills*

The case for yellow school buses

Sir Moir Lockhead OBE

Chief Executive of FirstGroup plc, wants to see high-quality transport for today's schoolchildren

I never travelled to school by bus but I'm now passionate in my desire to see more British children get to and from school on a dedicated service. Why didn't I catch a bus? In the County Durham mining village I grew up in the school was only five doors away from my house – although my brother and I used to spin out that short journey as long as we could.

Today's children more often live five miles, rather than five houses, from school. Even when they live much closer, today's parents are much less willing to allow their kids to walk than those of 10 or 20 years ago.

My first bus journey took me to my first job and since then buses have become my career. But in all that time I've never been more impressed by the great job buses can do for society than when I first saw American school buses in action. These iconic vehicles carry around 9 billion young passengers a year safely and securely to and from their local school.

In the home of the car, over half of America's children use yellow school buses. Sadly, in Britain only one in 20 of those attending primary school travels there by bus and the numbers of schoolchildren travelling by car has doubled in the last 20 years.

Now, more than ever before, the case for rolling out dedicated, high-quality home-to-school transport across Britain is overwhelming. The Yellow School Bus Commission's recent report argued the case and estimated that 180 million unnecessary car journeys would be removed from our streets as a result.

Like the Commission, I'd like to see more children cycle or walk to school as I used to. But where that's not practical then let's replace the school run with the yellow school bus.

Sir Moir Lockhead with one of the yellow school buses he has championed.

Silent, smooth and environmentally perfect

Peter M. D. Lutman

Consultant and former transport manager, went to school on a different type of yellow school bus

In 1951, the year when the last trams ran in Newcastle upon Tyne, I transferred at the age of 11 from a local Council School in Newcastle's west end near my home to a Grammar School in Jesmond, north east of the city centre. I was fortunate in two respects: the nearest services were operated by trolleybuses 200 metres from home and most linked across the city centre to Jesmond, 150 metres from school. With 16 trolleybuses per hour, 12 of which went to Osborne Road in Jesmond, the service was superb.

From the earliest age I can remember, I had been fascinated by public transport vehicles and their routes and I can still recall the withdrawal of the Elswick Road trams and their replacement in 1943 by utility Karrier trolleybuses. Occasionally, strange red trolleybuses would appear, hired from Brighton to relieve the pressure during World War 2.

Newcastle had, by 1951, 186 very new trolleybuses serving 20 routes (if you counted all the As, Bs and Cs variations); the prewar fleet worn out during the hostilities had been retired and the utility Karriers were parked up in the little-used Haymarket depot after just seven years of use. Like most British systems, there was virtually no integration between the routes served by trolleybuses and those covered by diesels. It would have been far more sensible to cover the basic frequency on more routes with the electric vehicles and to use the diesels to provide the peak-hour extra short-workings, returning empty against the peak flow by the most direct route.

It cost 2½d (1p) to get to or from school, but especially in the late afternoon the return journey was slow, impeded by selfish car parking on several busy city centre streets. Speed was also restricted by the eight junctions

Just out of service when Peter started travelling to school by trolleybus in Newcastle were the last of the prewar vehicles bought between 1935 and 1940 as the system grew. This is a 1939 Karrier E6A/Roe used on the 36 between Fenham and Central Station. *C. Carter*

at which the overhead wires bifurcated, crossed or joined, where the maximum speed was just 5mph (8kph). Newcastle's overhead was largely home-made, ugly, badly placed and with sharply angled points (frogs) so just occasionally with a crash and a bang the booms would part company with the overhead, requiring the conductor to pull out a long bamboo pole from a special tube on the bus to hook them back on the wires. When the Board of Trade inspected the routes they imposed ridiculously low speed limits (15 or 20 mph on parts of Elswick Road for example) details of which were posted in the depots and all of which were totally ignored by the drivers!

I used to hang around Wingrove trolleybus depot on some evenings and 'help' the yard-man by pulling the levers to change the points on the overhead to get the incoming trolleybuses on to their allotted bay. I got to know many crews as a result, so by the time I was 14 or 15 years old the conductor would grab me as I boarded the trolleybus to school and instruct me to 'watch the bells' as he or she could then issue the tickets unimpeded by the frequent stops.

The trolleybuses were luxurious; silent, smooth, very reliable, environmentally perfect and wonderful at climbing Newcastle's steep hills quickly, so of course they had to be withdrawn in 1966 (nine years after I left school) in a typical act of municipal vandalism. In over 1,260 days of travel to and fro the trolleybuses let me down just once, when the opening of a pair of new CEGB power stations at Stella caused a major short-circuit and cut all electric power to the whole city for much of the day. Let's hope the schoolchildren of Leeds will soon be able to enjoy the same pleasure I got from getting to and from school by trolleybus.

In at the deep end

Mark Lyons

Bus photographer, in London, Basingstoke and the south coast

My interest in buses goes back as far as I can remember. Early recollections, from the first years of my life in the Croydon area, are of the London Transport standards of the time – RTs, various types of Routemaster (including FRM1), RFs and the XA class Atlanteans which linked Croydon to the vast New Addington estate.

My view of the bus world at the time was very London-centric and I clearly remember how strange the buses in Bournemouth and east Devon, which we visited on family holidays, looked.

At the age of seven my father's employer relocated from central London to Basingstoke and we moved to a newly-built house on the south-western outskirts of the town. Officially designated a London overspill town, the Basingstoke of the early 1970s was undergoing rapid expansion to absorb the capital's excess population who were to be housed in a number of new estates around the edge of the north Hampshire market town. The roads and other infrastructure preceded the houses which is how I came to attend Manor Field Junior School which at the time sat surrounded by a series of fields, some of which still housed livestock, criss-crossed by a network of roads complete with lay-bys for yet-to-be-

Typical of the buses that transported Mark to his school swimming classes, Hants & Dorset Bristol LD/ECW no.425 lays over among similar vehicles at Basingstoke bus station. Although carrying cream NBC-style fleet names its Wilts & Dorset heritage is belied by the Tilling Red livery with twin cream relief lined out in black. It also carries the scars left by the removal of its WD fleet number plate and, like most of the town's buses, the front dome shows evidence of close encounters of the arboreal kind! *Dale Tringham*

introduced bus services. I walked through this bizarre landscape to and from school each day and watched as a vast housing estate rose from the fields to become Brighton Hill.

Most bus services in Basingstoke were in the hands of Hants & Dorset although much of the Wilts & Dorset heritage remained, not least the Tilling red livery, although the buses gained cream NBC-style fleet names in late 1972. The bulk of the fleet was standard Bristol/ECW Tilling fare, although there were still some rebodied Bristol Ls and a handful of ex-Maidstone & District Leylands – single-deck Panthers in Tilling red, also some very early Atlanteans which carried the somewhat anaemic early incarnation of NBC red. For some reason all of the double-deckers, even those fresh out of the paintshops, had battered front domes!

The lack of a suitable local route meant that our family made relatively little use of the bus other than occasional indulgence trips with my mother. That was until the school Head decided that we should all be taught how to swim. Like most primary schools we lacked a pool and arrangements were therefore made for us to attend weekly lessons in the local municipal pool. Basingstoke Sports Centre was situated in the shopping centre, a mid-1960s affair which spanned the valley of the River Loddon. The swimming pool was located under the complex and, with no natural daylight, was not an inviting prospect. Unbeknown to the

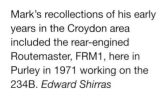

Mark's recollections of his early years in the Croydon area included the rear-engined Routemaster, FRM1, here in Purley in 1971 working on the 234B. *Edward Shirras*

An ex-Maidstone & District Leyland Panther/Willowbrook, new in 1967 and transferred to Wilts & Dorset in 1971, here in Basingstoke in 1973. *P. Richman*

school, however, for this pupil at least the plan had what would in today's parlance be described as a USP – we were going to have to take the bus. What's more, unlike other school trips for which the normal transport was a petrol-driven Bedford coach from either Porter of Dummer or Altonian, we were to be transported in a double-decker bus hired from Hants & Dorset. In an instant I became a committed swimmer.

And so it was that once a week a party of 60 or so children would gather in a lay-by yet to see regular bus services, sports bags in hand, for our swimming lessons. The bus provided was one that laid over between morning and afternoon peaks and was usually an early Bristol LD with conductor-operated platform doors. The teachers were doubtless perplexed at my enthusiasm for swimming lessons, particularly when compared to the supreme indifference I had for all other organised sporting activities. I usually conspired to bag one of the front seats on the upper deck.

The journey to the bus station lasted about 15 minutes but I was immersed in a world of my own, taking in the sights, smells and sounds from my green leatherette upholstered vantage point. All too soon the journey was over and a crocodile of small children would walk the 200 yards or so uphill to the sports centre. The lesson itself seemed to drag on interminably as we were forced through various stroke techniques and made to recover a rubber-coated brick from the base of the pool (why anyone would risk life and limb to rescue a brick is beyond me …) before we would retrace our steps.

Basingstoke bus station also housed the town's bus depot, which was mostly open parking. After a short interval one of the serried line of Bristol double-deckers would burst into life and draw up to the stand. Sixty schoolchildren, still all slightly damp from their recent swim, ensured that whatever the weather the inside of the bus quickly steamed up – as a consequence the journey back to school was undertaken accompanied by much writing of names in the condensation on the windows!

In the summer of 1975 it was announced that a service bus would be introduced to Brighton Hill. More importantly for me, the terminal point was the lay-by outside my school and so it came to pass that twice every hour a bus would draw up and stand in full view of the school playing fields. For some reason lost in the mists of time, for most of the 1970s Basingstoke's buses carried route numbers in the 400 series heading south and 300s heading north. So it was that during the layover the destination blinds and route number would be changed and what arrived as a 411 would become a 312 destined for Park Prewett, a rather forbidding Victorian asylum on the northern edge of the town. On the other half hour a 412 would arrive on the opposite side of the road and, after a few minutes, depart as a 311. Sadly, extension was accompanied by conversion to single-deck one-man (as it still was) operation, usually with Leyland Nationals, although the reality of bus operation at the time meant that just about anything fit for service would appear.

My school breaks were therefore spent blissfully watching a collection of buses comprising Bristol MWs and LHs (including the dual-door versions favoured by both the '& Dorset' companies for a while), the ex-M&D Panthers and of course the rattly Nationals, pass by. For some reason (probably

to take up some slack in the crew roster) the Sunday service, which did not start until early afternoon, was in the hands of Lodekkas.

At the age of 11 a change in my bus-watching activities was forced upon me by a change of school which was (almost literally) across the road from where we lived and did not really afford a decent view of buses from its grounds. The die had been well and truly cast, though, and I quickly found ways of getting a regular bus fix, something that has continued to this day. As to the swimming, well I did actually end up quite enjoying it, and eventually ended up learning how to scuba dive, an activity I continue with, albeit in waters considerably more inviting than a north Hampshire municipal swimming pool!

A newly-delivered Hants & Dorset Bristol VRT/ECW sits in Basingstoke next to a petrol-engined Bedford coach from the Porter of Dummer fleet that took Mark and his schoolmates on school trips. *P. R. Nuttall*

Musical Regents and unpleasant Leylands

Ian Manning

Transport manager, learned to love buses – and AECs in particular – during his Sheffield schooldays

I come from a non-car-owning household in a suburb of western Sheffield and was born in 1954. My first encounters with the bus were apparently in my pram when I used to get very excited at the mere sight of one. My own personal memories of my earliest experiences in life were from 1958 and 1959 and both involved buses.

The first, which was the most pronounced and long-lasting, involved standing at the

Ian age 9.

School Road bus shelter in Crookes with my uncle and watching the new fleet of 1957 AEC Regent V D3RVs go by, which had just replaced the trams. Even at this age I had discovered that there were two distinct sounds made by these buses, caused, I discovered much later in life, by the fact that some of them had gearboxes with hardened

gearwheels. This technical explanation of what is a musical phenomenon was to become my passion until the mid-1970s when every UK example had been eliminated from operational fleets.

The second early memory was of holidays to Shanklin, Isle of Wight, in those years where I saw and rode on my first open-top buses in the shape of the two 1939 Bristol K5Gs numbered 702 and 703. The link here is that I also rode on both of these buses in the month before writing this and I myself jointly own an open-top Bristol Lodekka!

So bearing in mind we went everywhere by bus, how did the school bus shape my thinking and for that matter my future life? Lydgate Lane Primary School was at the bottom of our garden but the third year of

The handsome batch of AEC Regent V/Weymann delivered as Sheffield nos.64-73 and later renumbered 264-273, did their second main stint of duty on service 51. No.267 is seen at the Lodge Moor Hospital terminus in June 1967. *G. Mead*

A Sheffield Leyland Farington-bodied Titan PD2/1 at the City terminus of the 54 and 55. No.610 had been transferred to Greenland Road Garage by the time of regular buses to school, leaving only no.620 as a regular Townhead Street bus from the batch on these routes. *Paul Fox collection*

the Junior School period there had to be spent at the Broomhill Annexe, just too far for a nine year old to walk and that meant four buses a day, because thankfully I never had to suffer school meals!

The first bus service on our road (I lived at the second highest point in the city) was introduced in April 1960 with a magnificent part batch of new AEC Regent V/Weymann (nos.451-45). However, using the excuse that the gradient of the car park terminus of the Norfolk Arms at Rivelin Dams was proving to be difficult for the reversing manoeuvre necessary for the Regents whose low floor platforms were prone to ground there (who said low-floor buses were a new phenomenon?), service 54, which only ran once an hour (twice at peaks), had been converted back to a 1954 batch of Leyland PD2/12 with Weymann bodies by the time I travelled to school by bus. I hated these because of their smelly clutches from the change down into second gear necessary to cope with the 1 in 7 gradient of our road!

For greater frequency for the school journey, I could either walk down to services 51 and 55 at Crosspool Shops or down to Crookes School Road for one of the aforementioned hallowed Regents on service 52, but the problem with the latter was that I had already walked half way to the school and would only enjoy just three short stops on the run to school. The Crosspool option, which was the shorter and less steep of the walks, brought me either one of the long Regents on the 51 from Lodge Moor or, my most hated buses of the time, one of two 1947 all-Leyland PD2/1s numbered 553 and 554 which seemed to alternate daily with monotonous regularity on service 55 which shuttled every half hour to and from the City Centre with most efficient schedules.

Regular unsupervised use of the bus enabled me to further engage my curiosity into how bus schedules worked. I had already taken to recording which adverts were placed on the sides and rears of each bus, so that if I was using service 54 I could usually have worked out from bedroom window observations which fleet number was going to come on my journey. Now it was possible to either stare through into the driver's cab to try and read the running boards. Better still, if the conductor had it, to wait until he went upstairs and then get it from behind the rear offside longitudinal seat and study, if not write down,

The first bus to operate over Lydgate Lane in April 1960, AEC Regent V/Weymann no.454 entered service that month and is seen at the Rivelin Dams reversal terminus in May 1961. Note the cast-iron bus stop and display case. The general manager's excuse about damaging the platform whilst reversing does not seem believable! *Paul Fox collection*

the required detail. I learnt that the bus that worked the afternoon and evening journeys had spent all the morning on a completely different route and that on the last journey to Crosspool at night it fell to the conductor to turn off the lights in the Manchester Road bus shelter! By the age of 10, I had decided to put this type of knowledge into practice and designed timetables, scheduled and finally produced my own running boards for my own company, Hercules Motor Services (Hercules was the model of my bike!).

One unfortunate incident in 1964 was getting stung in the head by a wasp that had found its way into my school cap in the cloakroom and stayed there before attacking me aboard PD2 no.687. The bus, unlike the wasp, lives on in preservation!

The primary school year raised enough interest in buses in my classmates (of which there were some 31 girls and another 16 boys – teachers' trade unions eat your hearts out!) that I actually established a small Bus Enthusiasts Club with a monthly newsletter produced by my draughtsman father. We even persuaded a teacher to head up a visit to Sheffield Transport's East Bank bus garage with trips round the workshop pits, a ride through the bus wash and a trip up to the withdrawn vehicle parking area, normally only

to be viewed at a distance through a fence from the main road! When I moved to King Edward VII Grammar School after one year back at the main Primary School building in 1965, the school journey was virtually identical, being just one stop further but effectively confining me more to the 54 and 55 routes to avoid more hill climbing on foot.

The 54 was still the smelly and characterless PD2/12s and the 55 still the ancient 553 and 554, all of which suddenly were replaced by first of all the reinstated survivors of the batch of Cravens-bodied preselect Regent IIIs (nos.243-249) and then in turn by the batch of lowbridge Regent III/Weymann (nos.1283-1291) rendered homeless by the roadworks to higher the bridge at South Anston on Services 6 and 19 on which they had worked.

Both types of vehicle were unpopular with the commuters and shoppers I travelled with, the Cravens buses because of their age and hasty reinstatement (the fleet names had even been painted out ready for disposal) and the latter for their lowbridge sunken side gangway configuration.

I discovered that these changes were because both routes were considered to be unprofitable and therefore were allocated the oldest vehicles (nobody told me about

A later all-Leyland Titan PD2, no.373, leaves the concealed bus shelter at the bottom of Manchester Road where the conductor had to turn off the lights as part of his bus duty on the last trip. *J. Howard Turner*

depreciation at that stage, but I have used that argument in response to many a complaint in professional life since).

However, a great change took place in 1968 when Townhead Street garage, which operated the 51, 54 and 55, shut and the services were restructured. The 55 was abandoned altogether and replaced by more journeys on the 54 over my road, which suited me even better, but the route was to become operated by Leadmill garage using the surviving PD2/ Weymann but now supplemented by the Weymann Orion-bodied AEC Regent IIIs and Vs, two of which (nos.751 and 792) still had their most musical rarer gearboxes. Add to this the fact that the best of them all, 790, was frequently to be found on the Inner Circle which also passed the school and could enliven a Physics or Art lesson (the two subjects I hated!) as it sang its way up Newbould Lane.

The Outer Circle service 2 was also diverted to serve my school at the same time, whilst service 51 was transferred to Greenland garage and by then was largely operated by the last batch of Regent V/Weymann with front entrances and by then numbered 264-273. These buses featured in my school itinerary every Wednesday, because to avoid games (my only other hatred at school), I participated with others in Youth Action and I went to visit Britain's then longest surviving iron lung patient and a geriatric ward at Lodge Moor Hospital, which I considered to be a very

No.687 was a Leyland Titan PD2/12/Weymann which replaced trams on the Ecclesall routes and later came to the 54 and 55. This one was identical to the one that was the location where Ian was stung in the head by the wasp. *Alan B. Cross*

Surviving Cravens-bodied AEC Regent IIIs ended their days at Townhead Street on the 51/54/55. No.245 rests on Pond Street bus station park on the part-day vehicle working on the 51. *Paul Fox collection*

constructive way of spending time otherwise condemned to be spent chasing a spherical or oval shaped piece of leather in exposed locations where it rained horizontally.

The school playing fields at Whitely Woods and Castle Dyke were also a three-mile journey from the school and brought a great variety of vehicles with which to transport us. The skill was to get on what I wanted and not necessarily the bus to which I was directed! All depots participated in the provision of the facility and the buses that took us to the sites did not necessarily bring us back; the pleasure was only in the transport, but not always if you ended up with one of the lower streams whose pupils always seemed to be the rowdies who caused trouble and needed supervision when boarding the Inner Circle routes which provided other bulk movements of scholars to my school.

By the time I left school, the 51 had been converted to AEC Swifts (driver-only) and the 2/54 was working a complex seven-hour cycle from Herries Garage with unpleasant new 33ft-long Leyland Atlantean/Park Royals, but also with a couple of Leadmill operated workings that could usually be relied upon to produce a conventional bus.

The bus to school that Ian loved to hate: 1947 all-Leyland PD2/1 no.554, showing the scars of its hasty reinstatement with three unpainted panels without the red lining, in Campo Lane on the Wisewood route. No doubt no.553 was on service 55 on that day. *J. Howard Turner*

My conclusion in relation to the influence of the school bus in later life is that it had already bestowed upon me the gift of scheduling, the facility to see good and bad crews at work and to evaluate the merits and demerits of different types of vehicles. I had an indelible hatred of badly-behaved schoolkids both waiting for and on board buses that always made me feel embarrassed. I already held a strong view that schoolchildren should travel on normal service buses (a nearby Catholic school had dedicated contract buses, despite being in an urban area on a frequent network route).

When I left school to study German, French and Linguistics at Edinburgh University, I had no thoughts of joining the bus industry even though there were other enthusiasts at the school and we often went off together for the day on Saturdays or in the holidays to travel round the country on buses in as far as our pocket money and parental leashes allowed it. Curiously my current Cheltenham depot manager ended up marrying a girl he met on his school bus!

Today I have no love of transporting schoolchildren and have spent my career gradually dispensing with so-called 'commercial' school buses provided to transport non-entitled children at peak times at discounted rates for more obscure movements on urban networks to prevent them changing buses at town/city centres. When such buses only perform for 190 days of the year, they are unlikely to make money unless permanently full and charging pretty high fares with angelically-behaved kids, which is an all too rare combination.

I got totally fed up with the seat-belt campaigners of the 1990s when in local authority transport and I am probably not actively sympathetic enough to the view that we should give the best possible view of the industry to those at an impressionable age to ensure that they do not rush off and buy cars at the first available opportunity. In truth, such a campaign would now probably prove quite worthwhile, given changing attitudes to the environment. What we must do, however, is to positively present our industry to young people to find more schedulers, service designers, operatives and future managers from our schools to provide future generations of passionate managers to replace the very high proportion of us now in our fifties!

The buses that inspired Ian's interest! The 1957 Regent V/Weymanns that replaced the trams on the 52 exemplified by no.789 heading up High Street on the short-working to School Road. This one had the gearbox with hardened gearwheels when new. Note the arm indicators, which were fairly quickly replaced. It is passing one of the 35 Roberts trams built between 1950 and 1952.
Alan B. Cross

'By the banks of my own lovely Lee'

Cyril McIntyre

Retired bus manager and transport author, on school journeys in Cork

I was born in 1943 in Cork city, where my father was based as an inspector attached to the Omnibus Department of the Great Southern Railways. He had started his transport career in 1931 as a conductor with the Irish Omnibus Company, then a subsidiary of the GSR and fully absorbed in 1934. After his promotion to Inspector in 1936 he worked in Waterford and Galway before transferring to Cork in 1940.

With that family background I suppose it was inevitable that I would develop an interest in transport and especially in buses. We lived at Glenbrook, a little over seven miles outside the city, on the western shore of Cork Harbour. One of my earliest memories is of seeing a red-and-white bus with what seemed to me to be a long bonnet parked outside our house on Glenbrook Terrace. The road widened slightly at this location; it was a convenient point for 'auxiliary' or duplicate buses to turn after transferring their few remaining passengers and then await the next

service to the city from Monkstown or Ringaskiddy. Years later I learned that this bus must have been a Leyland Cub 20-seater of the former GSR fleet, acquired by CIE in the 1945 amalgamation of the GSR with the Dublin United Transport Company.

There were occasional bus trips to and from Cork during my pre-school years, but it was when I started school in 1948 that I became a daily bus user. The school was located in Monkstown, about 1½ miles further south on the road to Ringaskiddy. So every morning I boarded the Cork/Ringaskiddy service bus at the regular stopping place (no bus stop signs on country routes in those days) across the road from Glenbrook Terrace. The fact that children as young as five travelled unaccompanied to school by ordinary service bus, which would be unheard of nowadays, reflects the innocent way of life of a bygone era in Ireland.

The journey was quite short, following the course of the river Lee as it broadened out

It's 1948 and Cyril and his sister Bernadette at the bus stop (former railway station) in Monkstown; the school across the road is just visible at the left of the photo. The bus is CIE TF11, a Leyland Tiger with a four-cylinder engine of the former GSR fleet dating from 1937. In the background is the trackbed of the former Cork Blackrock & Passage Railway, closed in 1932.

It's 2006 and Cyril is at the wheel of a new Mercedes Eurocoach school bus delivered to Bus Éireann in August that year, just two months before he retired.

into Cork Harbour. Ships passing to and from the port of Cork could be seen from the bus, as well as trains on the railway line to Cobh on the opposite side of the river. The single fare for the journey was 1d; I accumulated quite a collection of white 1d tickets, none of which alas survive in my ticket collection today. I recall being fascinated by the 'rack' of multi-coloured tickets which the conductor carried and, of course, observed closely the working of the distinctive Williamson bell punch of the time.

As the school in Monkstown was an offshoot of the convent school in Passage West, the previous stage on the route, the two nuns who taught all classes were also regular passengers on the morning bus. Among the other children who travelled were the two Carpenter girls, Avril and Yvonne, whose father owned the Club Hotel located between Passage West and Glenbrook. On the return journey in mid-afternoon the nuns were invariably missing, as they stayed back to prepare work for the following day and got a later bus. However, the regular conductors could always be relied on to stop at Glenbrook Terrace where I alighted.

The buses on which I travelled to and from school were invariably former GSR Leyland Tigers with 32-seater bodies, dating

from the 1930s and all now painted in the green livery of CIE; some of the fleet numbers I remember were TP63, TP65, TF1 and TF11. Very occasionally one of the T class would appear on the route; these were Leyland Tiger TS11 chassis delivered in 1942 but not placed in service until 1947 after bodying by CIE. As they were not fitted with roof luggage carriers they spent most of their time on city services. A real treat in October 1948 was a trip on P16; this was one of the first of the new Leyland Tiger OPS3 39-seaters to be allocated to the Cork depot, heralding a major postwar fleet replacement programme.

In February 1951 we moved to Mayfield on the north side of Cork city. Here the school was only five minutes walk from our house so going by bus to school became a thing of the past. However, on starting secondary school in 1956 I again became a daily bus traveller, this time on city services. Here the TIM ticket machine reigned supreme, but still printing tickets with GSR and even IOC titles; the country service conductors who worked peak-hour extras had by now graduated to the Setright Speed and the bell punches were just a childhood memory.

City service buses were invariably Leyland double-deckers, a mixture of Titan TD5, TD7 and OPD2 types. There were, however, four TD4 vehicles with GSR bodies dating from 1936 (R247-250), usually confined to peak-hour extras, so now the treat for me was to travel on them as often as possible before they would soon disappear. Many a time I waited for a later journey to sample their unique ambience, before they were finally withdrawn in 1958.

Little did I realise during those days of travelling by bus to school that I would later spend my entire working life in transport, much of it dealing with buses. I joined CIE as a junior clerk in 1961, moved to Bus Éireann in the re-organisation of the CIE Group in 1987 and retired as Manager Fleet Planning & Control of Bus Éireann in 2006. But it all started 'by the banks of my own lovely Lee' travelling by bus to school in Monkstown …

Rugby's saving grace

Alan Millar

Editor of Buses magazine, remembers his Glasgow schooldays

I am just old enough and was born in the right place for my bus to school having sometimes been a tram.

Hillhead Primary, where my formal education began in August 1959, is in the West End of Glasgow, about four stops by corporation bus or tram from Woodlands Road, the secondary thoroughfare nearest by childhood home. Trams continued in that part of town until June 1960, so there was a chance for most of my first school year of catching either a number 10 tram or an 11 bus, whichever came first.

Thinking back, it strikes me either how safe things were perceived to be 50 years ago or how foolhardy or confident my parents were, for I realise that although my mother accompanied me on the first day to

12 year-old Alan in school uniform (cap in hand) in 1966, looking calm in spite of the prospect of weekly rugby practice.

school and probably for some time afterwards, she certainly trusted me to make the journey on my own by public transport long before the end of that first school year, being satisfied that once seen aboard a bus or tram, nothing could go wrong.

I know this because I still recall my sense of panic on the first occasion I made the journey alone by tram. The enthusiast in me even remembers that it was a Cunarder, the last new design of tram built by Glasgow Corporation between 1948 and 1952. The panic was because buses and trams stopped at separate stops, orangey-yellow ones for buses, red ones for trams; the ones where bus fares changed were called Fare Stage, while those for a tram said Fare Station.

Glasgow Corporation A25, a Crossley-bodied AEC Regent III that served the city from 1948 to 1966, in Knightswood Garage after operating route 11. *Jim Thomson*

I knew exactly where to get off the bus on the Great Western Road, but the equivalent tram stop must have been a lamp-post or two earlier and I found myself being propelled – probably displaying visible signs of alarm to the conductress – westwards to a mysterious land of who knows where. Actually, it was only a block of tenements away and within easy reach of school, albeit that it meant crossing the side road in which the school remains today. Nonetheless, this made me wary of trams, although I guess I used them again before they disappeared.

The 11 bus was and remained my main transport to and from school until a domestic deal let me have access to the fares as pocket money in exchange for walking to school, though I continued to use buses to get home and back at lunch time. The fare over those first years was one-and-a-half old pence each way – a 'three-ha'penny half' in the words of one English conductor on the route – issued as a beige-coloured Ultimate ticket with the boarding fare stage printed in purple in the 'CHILD' box in the bottom right-hand corner of the ticket, next to the other box titled 'ORD'. When fares did rise, there was always

the mild excitement of wondering in what different colour the new versions were printed.

Most buses on this route were AEC Regents, a mix of MkIIIs with exposed radiators and three styles of bodywork, and MkVs with concealed radiators, Gardner 6LW engines and one style of bodywork. I should add that I know a lot more of these facts now than I did in 1959, 1960 or until a truly wonderful Ian Allan *abc* on Glasgow Corporation Transport enlightened me around 1964 on these and many other technical facts.

Pre-school, I identified them by the sounds they made. MkIIIs were 'ah-oom' buses, MkVs 'Vaagh' and in hopefully private moments (eg not on the bus to school) I imitated said noises to my own satisfaction and delight.

The MkIIIs' bodies were mainly by Metro-Cammell or Weymann to a Met-Cam design also found, I discovered much later, with Leicester and Red & White. But there were two other distinct batches, one of 20 by Northern Coach Builders and one of 50 by Crossley, which seemed particularly handsome and for some unaccountable reason I have always felt looked feminine, like a mature aunt. Don't ask me why.

The MkVs, which I regarded less fondly because of the relative harshness of the sounds they emitted, were truly unusual vehicles that all vanished into the oblivion that met most buses before the preservation movement took root. Glasgow had 75 of them, all with a prewar design of preselector gearbox, a grille with slats cut out and a five-bay pre-Orion body from Weymann. Except that although Weymann built 26 of them, the other 49 were built by Alexander to Weymann's design and probably largely with Weymann parts.

These journeys started to provide me with more of the knowledge and interest in buses that has enriched (or blighted?) my life ever since. For some buses had plates inside to say whose bodies they carried – MCCW, MCW, Weymann or Alexander on transmission cowls or little plastic badges screwed into the front bulkhead downstairs. They also had A-prefixed fleet numbers that I long thought stood for ABC until I eventually read them properly as AEC after a closer look at a radiator badge. Some also had Regent badges.

I also began to recognise that some buses were different from most, having a saloon heater downstairs and an opening window behind the driver's cab. Much later, I learnt that these were the vehicles bought to provide night services beyond midnight on a few routes (hence the heaters) and that the opening windows were for daytime use by the driving school. As I recall, the obvious external differences of the NCB and Crossley bodies were accompanied by internal distinctions like horizontally-ribbed material on the lower panels of the front bulkhead of the former and relatively low seats – in relation to the windows – on the Crossley bodies.

One day – and I hoped against impossible hope that there would be another – my number 11 was like no other I caught before or after. A single-decker. Glasgow was one of those places where single-deck corporation buses (and trams) ran only where bridges were too low. You chanced upon them in obscure suburban parts or on private hires. Knightswood Garage, which operated the 11, had a few at the time for a short route in the north of the city, and it was one of these – a Daimler CVD6 with Corporation-built body – that appeared magically one blissful morning. Besides the obvious difference of there being no stairs or top deck, the added thrill was its possession of two doors and I seem to recall being ushered out by the back after boarding by the front. But that may be imagination.

Before my school bus travel days ended, there were times when I broke the rules and used other routes. Much as I would crave a ride in any of those Regents today, they got boring and the CVD6 single-decker never returned. The 10 tram was withdrawn

A158, a 1950 AEC Regent III with Metro-Cammell body, working an eastbound journey on the 11 in June 1961. It is in the later Glasgow livery of top half green, bottom half yellow. After withdrawal in 1966 it served for a time as a snowplough, clearing bus routes in winter. *G. Mead*

Cunarder tram no.1378, similar to those operated on Glasgow route 10.
Jim Thomson

without replacement, but Daimler double-deckers with a variety of shapes and sound effects arrived to replace the 3 tram along Woodlands Road. So there was an occasional attraction of catching one of these to Glasgow University and walking a little farther to school, especially while truly musical CWA6s were among them.

Walking farther at the home end and catching one of the busy routes that ran only along Great Western Road opened up further possibilities, like rides on new-fangled Leyland PD3s and Regent Vs with forward entrances and driver-operated folding doors (air on the Leylands, electric on the AECs) – the sort of schoolboy behaviour that greatly irritated conductors when you clearly let older buses sail past and then stuck your hand out at the last minute to stop one with doors. Both types, in truth, were utilitarian and rough by almost any measure, but the MkVs especially appealed thanks to the sound effects of their AEC engines and Monocontrol gearboxes.

Such a journey involving a longer walk was irresistible one lunchtime when the truly revolutionary LA1 rolled up at the school bus stop on its direct route into town. This was like no other bus I had ever seen before, for it not only had doors, but these were at the very front next to the driver and its engine was at the back. It just had to be sampled and, besides its different internal layout, it offered sound effects that convinced me the letters in its fleet number stood for Leyland AEC, for it somehow had qualities of both makes. I would later banish such an idiotic notion, learning that A was for Atlantean.

It was on a journey to school one morning in 1962 that something even more amazing caught my eye, in Woodlands Road, on its way towards the city in the opposite direction. This was something like LA6 – I don't remember its exact identity for sure – but this was among the first of the hundreds of Atlanteans that flowed into the fleet for the rest of the 1960s. Besides its layout, this brought transatlantic styling of Ford Consul Classic proportions to my corporation buses, for glassfibre and curved glass gave it big moulded windows and imaginative shaped panels at the front. This was the future. And it was here.

By the time I started secondary school in 1966, Atlanteans were as old hat as half-cab AECs and, indeed, the Regent IIIs were reaching the end of their lives. Hillhead High was nearer home and within walking distance at lunch time, so I walked there all the time. Except that a new aspect of the week came with the move to the 'big school'. Monday afternoon rugby practice.

I truly hated that experience. My inclination was to put myself anywhere on the field that saved me the embarrassment and potential indignity of not knowing what to do with the ball. I have every admiration for those who enjoy and are good at team sports, as long as they don't want me to be part of the process.

But the saving grace was that it was sandwiched between two bus rides that did as much as anything to invigorate and maintain my enthusiasm to this day. The Corporation hired coaches to take us to the playing fields at Garscadden on the western edge of the city, but left us to find our own way home by scheduled bus.

To begin with, the coaches were coaches, mostly 41-seat Ford Thames Traders with Duple Yeoman or newer bodywork. But after a few months, or maybe by our second year, old double-deckers took their place from companies like Northern Roadways, which had a lot, and some smaller fleets of only two or three vehicles.

Northern Roadways bought whole batches from Scottish Bus Group fleets and painted them in approximations of its green livery. There were Leyland PD1s from Central SMT and Western SMT, which displayed their age and decrepitude through the sound effects of well-worn axles, propshafts or gearboxes, as well as – by its standards – 'modern' Guy Arab IVs, whose original sound effects were hard to beat, and helped soften my dread of the sports torture to come.

As they had open platforms, teachers and perhaps school prefects rode shotgun to prevent over-exuberant 12 and 13 year-olds falling off, but other double-deckers had doors. I recall an ex-North Western exposed radiator PD2 and a London RTL, but my favourite without question was an ex-Southdown all-Leyland PD2/12 with the final style of Leyland body we have learned in recent times not to call a Farington. Its special feature was not only having platform doors at the back, but electric ones controlled by the driver. This was luxury, for SBG's many buses of similar layout had manual doors operated by the muscular strength of often-formidable clippies.

The recommended bus home was by a corporation number 6, which terminated close to the playing fields. I recall such a journey being one of the other occasions when I had the fortune of riding aboard LA1, but the drawback was that although this removed me from the scene of torture, I had to change en route. If I walked a bit farther from the playing fields, I could catch my old friend the number 11.

The journey was a lot longer than when I had caught it to primary school, but not generally memorable. Except on 5 June 1967. I only recall the date because someone's evening newspaper headline read '*It's War*', for this was the first day of the Six-Day War between Israel and Egypt and I guess, not having been exposed to much war in my short lifetime, it was a bit worrying.

The bus was fairly new LA331, which tells you how mundane the futuristic had become by then, and as it entered the dual carriageway at route 11's western extremity of Great Western Road there was a loud bang or crunch. We had collided with a car alongside, inflicting enough damage to the panel below the driver's cab for the journey to be aborted. In the overall scheme of bus crashes, this was trivial. The bus lived another 12 years and for all I know had several other bumps and bashes or maybe none. But this was My Crash and I regarded LA331 thereafter as part of my life, to be acknowledged silently but knowingly when our paths crossed in future. And even that day it swept me away from the horrors of the rugby field.

The jinx bus and cold knees

Jasper Pettie

Noted bus preservationist, on his younger days in Western SMT territory

In 1953 when I was eight years old we moved from Perthshire to Ayrshire, an event that was to have a profound effect on my life in every respect.

I was already what you might call a dyed-in-the-wool 'bus spotter'. Although my first school in the village of Scone just outside Perth was within walking distance of our house, my mother would meet me at the school gates after lessons and we'd catch the bus into Perth to go shopping before teatime. These journeys were the start of a lifelong fascination for me of buses.

My parents spent some considerable effort selecting a school they felt suitable to develop and hone my nascent academic abilities and so I was duly packed off to Belmont House School in Newton Mearns near Glasgow, a distance of 12 miles from the village of Fenwick, just off the main A77 road, where we lived. In common with many families in the 1950s we did not possess a car

and thus there was no alternative but to travel courtesy of the local bus operator, Western SMT.

Fenwick was well served by the smart red-and-cream buses of 'the Western'. The most frequent was the Glasgow (Waterloo Street)-Ayr via Kilmarnock service, every 20 minutes, with duplicates at peak times, which included my school journey time. I discovered that three depots – Ayr, Newton Mearns and Kilmarnock – provided the bulk of the vehicle requirement for this route.

To reach school in time for the dreaded 9am bell meant I had to be at the stop outside the King's Arms Hotel at the top of our road to catch the 8.07, which was an Ayr depot duty running through from that town, hotly pursued by a duplicate from Kilmarnock. My steed on that very first day, and indeed the regular bus for many months, was brand-new AY1010 (ESD 208), Western's first Guy Arab IV and first 'tin-

The 'jinx bus', Western SMT's first Guy Arab IV/Northern Counties, AY1010 was a regular on Jasper's school run; it is seen here at Ayr bus station. *R. F. Mack*

front' with handsome Northern Counties 53-seat (27/26) lowbridge body, one of a batch of seven. AY1010 (**A**yr Gu**Y**) was destined to be the only one of the batch on this route but also my school run was the only journey it performed – this particular duty returned to Ayr from Glasgow via Troon instead of Kilmarnock on which it ran for the rest of the day.

On mornings when 1010 was unavailable almost any specimen of Ayr's finest could put in an appearance. The 16 1949 Albion Venturer CX37s with Alexander lowbridge 53-seat (27/26) bodies were Ayr's regular contribution to the route at this time along with the last (1946) Guy Arab IIs with highbridge Northern Counties 56-seat (30/26) bodies to the 'relaxed utility' style. This was a not infrequent occasion and as I got to know the regular conductresses (as they were called at that time – nobody had heard of 'clippies') I would ask where 1010 was, to be told 'Oh aye, that's the jinx bus – aff the road again!' I never did find out whether 1010 had inherently serious shortcomings but I suspect minor niggles seemed to plague it, like the bitterly cold morning when halfway across the Fenwick Moor the windscreen wiper motor packed up in driving sleet. Progress was halted while the driver phoned Newton Mearns depot from a nearby farm steading to request assistance. Fortunately the sleet abated and we were able to proceed somewhat gingerly to Mearns depot where after the maintenance staff had pronounced 1010's wiper motor beyond redemption we transferred to a Leyland PD1 for the last three stops to my school. The PD1 had sat out all night and the shock of transferring from our cosy conveyance to the PD1's arctic interior sticks out in my mind to this day! Some explaining was also necessary to account for our late arrival at school which, thankfully, proved sufficient to avoid

punishment (in those days, very likely of a corporal nature).

As mentioned above, Kilmarnock depot provided a duplicate running to Glasgow and returning to Kilmarnock only. The bus provided was almost invariably a Daimler, Kilmarnock sharing with Johnstone depot Western's entire Daimler fleet. Two buses are remembered as being regulars, KR917 (XS 7023) ,a 1950 CVG6/Northern Counties highbridge 56-seater, one of a batch ordered by Youngs of Paisley but delivered new to Western, and KR381 (BCS 440), a 1948 CVA6/Northern Counties lowbridge 53-seater of a batch of 28 CVA6s all allocated to Kilmarnock depot. The two KRs (**K**ilmarnock Daimle**R**) could not have been more different. No.917 was like a majestic galleon, with its 6LW purring, gliding smoothly across the Moor, whilst in complete contrast 381's AEC 7.7 engine thumped and banged to give a most unpleasant sensation in forward motion. Unfortunately this characteristic extended to the other 27 CVA6s and despite Western having a rich variety of bus makes at this time these must have been candidates for the most uncomfortable buses in the fleet.

After I had settled in at school a short time later I discovered I could sample a different delight if I got to the bus stop a few minutes earlier. The 7.56am Dumfries-Glasgow also passed through Fenwick and, Cumnock depot-operated, would produce a smart AEC Regent III, the full Monty version with 9.6-litre engine and preselective transmission. Yet, body-wise, these were identical to the Daimler CVA6s and shared an AEC engine – but what a difference to travel on! Smooth forward motion in contrast to the Daimlers' thumps and jerks, one didn't mind so much having to stand all the way …

And this was a feature of bus travel that I well remember from this time. Despite the frequency I sometimes found myself occupying the very last seat if I was lucky; if not it meant standing all the way across Fenwick Moor with not a hope of a seat until Mearns Cross was reached. Add to that the prospect of snow and ice in winter, and the open platforms, legs in short trousers could get very 'chapped' by the time of arrival!

The return journey after school was quite a different experience. The stop was on Fenwick Road on the A77 at the bottom of Sandringham Avenue and most buses that passed it were running only as far as Newton Mearns (where the depot was) or were turning left at Mearns Cross for Mearnskirk. Most Belmont schoolboys lived locally and thus used these services, but when an Ayr-bound bus was spotted in the distance those of us travelling beyond the Cross had to resort to drastic means to get the driver to stop, usually by standing in the middle of the road with arm outstretched to the limit! We became adept at recognising destinations on buses away in the distance – as well as Ayr or Ayr via Kilmarnock, buses to Girvan, Stranraer, Cumnock, Dumfries and Kilmarnock all passed through Fenwick, although many of these operated infrequently.

I used to dread Ayrshire public holidays. Bank holidays in Scotland were (and are) just that. Only the banks close but on certain Mondays throughout the year holidays take place on a local basis. Thus, for example on a Glasgow public holiday buses heading for Ayr and Troon would be full of trippers heading for the seaside in the morning, returning in the evening. But on Ayrshire public holidays many folk travelled to Glasgow for their day out and as they were making their way home at the same time as we were from school we were

Jasper's 'majestic galleon', Western SMT KR917, a 1950 Daimler CVG6/Northern Counties, one of six ordered by Young's, Paisley, but delivered new to Western following the takeover.

The full Monty – one of Cumnock depot's 1950 batch of AEC Regent III/Northern Counties, seen when new. Jasper didn't mind so much having to stand all the way on one of these. *A. B. Cross*

often treated to bus after bus speeding past loaded to the gunwhales, including duplicates only laid on for the day. We sometimes waited for hours and I remember on one occasion being rescued by the local coal merchant who just happened to be passing and we piled on to the back of his Bedford lorry amid the nutty slack! My mother was more grateful to see me home safe and sound rather than to give me a row about the state of my school uniform! I do believe my father lodged an official complaint with 'the Western' but bus companies generally took a rather more cavalier attitude to their passengers in the 1950s than today and nothing more was heard.

Afternoon journeys home tended to be

A 1955 Western Guy Arab LUF/Alexander – Jasper recalls a 'disastrous experiment' with some of these as part of Ayr's contribution to the Glasgow road, but after they had left passengers stranded at bus stops 'common sense prevailed'.

on Mearns depot Leyland PD1s, usually with ECW bodies some three years newer than the chassis. However on a Friday as we got out earlier I was able to catch a Stranraer-bound journey which I later learned was at 87 miles a candidate for the longest regular service anywhere in the UK operated by double-deckers. The regular steed at the time was AY191 (ASD 253), a 1943 Guy Arab whose body is still the subject of some controversy. Originally by Massey, it is reputed to have been rebuilt or rebodied at Western's Kilmarnock workshops and it had a distinctly Leyland-like appearance although the Massey cab structure had been retained.

As 1954 rolled into 1955 and 1956 inevitably some of the older buses were replaced with brand-new ones. The first tin-front Leyland PD2s were seen in 1955, with Northern Counties bodywork, operated from Newton Mearns, which heralded the eventual demise of variety. After a disastrous experiment with 44-seat Guy Arab LUF

single-deckers as part of Ayr's contribution to the Glasgow road had left scores of passengers stranded at bus stops common sense prevailed and smart new Guy Arab IVs with first Northern Counties and then Alexander bodies appeared in 1956/57. Cumnock also went single-deck for a while for its Glasgow-Dumfries allocation, providing AEC Regal IVs cascaded from the London service and reseated as buses. But the writing was on the wall. More PD2s and then PD3s swept away the opposition and by the time I moved on to boarding school in 1958 had virtually taken over all but the occasional journey.

My travelling-to-school days were over and now, a boarder, I was well and truly incarcerated for the next four long years. But what a difference the local bus scene made! SMT's Musselburgh depot was full of AECs and Leylands of seemingly ancient origin – but that's another story!

A penny one, please

Peter Rowlands

Transport journalist, dreams of schooldays in Newcastle upon Tyne

Somebody came with me on the bus on my first day at my first school in 1954: presumably my mother, though I couldn't swear to it. But never again; after that fleeting initiation at five years old, I was on my own. It's hard to imagine such apparent insouciance now, in this protective and politically-correct age, but back then it was nothing more than the norm.

The young Peter contemplates a career in journalism.

Instead, I was given a Puck matchbox with two old pennies in it, and instructed to ask the conductor: 'Can I have a penny one please?' Which I suppose I did, at first anyway. But I never heard anyone else ever recite this awkward formula, and pretty soon I modified it to something less naive. However, the matchbox routine lasted a few months before I decided that pockets would serve just as well.

The young Peter's 10-minute ride to school was on an exposed-radiator Brush-bodied Guy Arab III double-decker in the dark maroon livery of Gateshead & District – 'a grave-looking bus'.

The 10-minute ride was on an exposed-radiator Brush-bodied Guy Arab III double-decker in the rather sombre dark maroon livery of Gateshead & District. I didn't know the technical stuff at the time, of course; I just knew this was a grave-looking bus, with what seemed to me a rather tuneless engine (a Gardner, I assume) which emitted an inexplicable whistle when the driver took his foot off the throttle. It was 'the bus I went to school on', and that really said it all.

Some of the Guys I caught, I've since realised, had bodywork by Park Royal rather than Brush, although I honestly don't remember differentiating between the two types. Considering that I normally noticed every nuance of any bus I encountered, this now seems to me a rather remarkable failure of observation. I can only assume that my negative feelings towards these particular buses blinded me to their details.

I lived in Gosforth, on the northern fringes of Newcastle upon Tyne, and my journey took me slightly further north, to Coxlodge. In view of that, you might wonder why a Gateshead bus would have any part to play in my school travel.

The explanation is that Newcastle Corporation Transport and BET subsidiary Gateshead & District interworked on several cross-Tyne routes, and no fewer than five of these passed the end of my street: the 24, 25, 28, 29 and 30. Three terminated at North Kenton and environs, which was no good for my school, but the other two (the 24 and the 30) headed for Fawdon, a bit beyond Coxlodge.

My target bus was a 24, which got me to school comfortably in time for the 9am start. However, if I chanced to arrive at the stop a bit earlier, I could get the previous bus, a 30, which was run by yellow Northern Coachbuilders-bodied AEC Regent IIIs from the Newcastle Transport fleet.

These were altogether a different proposition. This model of Regent, from Newcastle's final 1950 batch, became my lifelong Favourite Bus of All Time. It had a delightfully musical engine and transmission (a crash box, I later discovered), and an altogether cheerful aura about it. Its presence on a school journey was an anomaly I was more than happy to tolerate.

I invariably travelled downstairs, having at some point concluded that the journey was too short to merit a trip to the upper deck – much as I would have preferred it, despite the cigarette smoke. There was also a sense that a trip to school did not merit celebrating, rather enduring. This meant I had plenty of chance to note whether the driver had pulled the blind down behind him (a dark magenta colour on the Regents, something unmemorable but even darker on the Guys), blocking the forward view into the half-cab through the bulkhead window. I always thought drivers who did this rather introverted and mean-spirited, though wonder now if in their place I would have done the same.

Early experience of these and similar buses exposed me to various mysteries. Why were some tickets available to 'WRKMN'? Who were these strange species who merited different fares from everyone else? And why were there notices inside the upstairs front windows saying that spitting was prohibited? Who would want to spit anyway? Why? This was an ugly if slightly oblique introduction into the behaviour of 'other people'.

Some buses (not necessarily mine) displayed the warning 'Standing and spitting prohibited'. Some wag invariably erased the 'p' in spitting, posing the question of how else one might contrive to travel: a childish joke that still makes me smile.

I also used to puzzle over the bland announcement displayed inside the Regent cabs above the driver's windscreen: 'This bus is 8ft wide.' I remember it being beautifully

typeset in what I now know is Gill Sans. Why did the driver need this information? It was only years later that I realised most buses up to that time had been 7ft 6in wide, and the drivers had to be encouraged not to point the Regents through gaps too narrow for them.

My bus turned right at the end of Ashburton Road (our local shopping street), proceeded down Salters Road as far as Jubilee Road, then took a left and continued towards Fawdon. Just before reaching my school it took a detour to the left along a half-crescent called Welford Avenue, which is where I alighted, walking down a short alley between meagre gardens to the back entrance to the school. The bus then turned right down Coxlodge Road (long since blocked off by a new road system) to rejoin Jubilee Road.

And here's the weird thing: I have strong memories of arriving at the school, with its pervasive smell of milk: crates gently warming against heating pipes during winter, giving me a lifelong aversion to it. But I have practically no memories of catching the bus home, or indeed arriving there and walking back up our street. Yet I must have done this daily for three years – except on occasional summer days, when my friend David and I would walk home the back way along Kenton Road, and spend the bus fare on sweets.

Peter hated prep school rugby, but loved the United ECW-bodied Bristol Ls that took him there.

By Bus to School

Peter's lifelong Favourite Bus of All Time was the Newcastle Corporation AEC Regent III with locally-built Northern Coachbuilders bodywork and 'an altogether cheerful aura about it'. It is here, appropriately, on route 30.

Neither the Guys nor the Regents were in fact the most common buses on my local routes – an honour that (in my memory at least) went to all-Leyland PD2s, which were operated by both Newcastle and Gateshead. But for some reason these never seemed to be allocated to the routes I used at the times I used them. Other buses often seen on local routes included 7ft 6in Regents with NCB and Massey bodies, and what seemed ancient Mann Egerton-bodied Daimlers.

After three years I moved to a preparatory school closer to my home, and was able to make the journey to and from it on foot (later by bike). However, this school too had its transport excitements in store – notably the pair of buses hired three times a week to take us to McCracken Park, the Northern Football Club rugby ground, out on the Great North Road. These, throughout my time there, were Bristol L single-deckers of United Automobile Services.

I hated the rugby – a phobia I'm pleased to say I finally put to rest years later, when I'd moved on to my final school. At the time, being pitched from the warmth of the buses to an often cold, alien rugby ground was simply another assault to be endured. And it was compounded by my anxiety about remembering which of the two buses I came

on. I always expected to get left behind one day, though I never was.

Yet I loved the buses themselves – the tuneful engine and gearbox, the beautifully proportioned ECW halfcab bodywork, the vivid red United livery, which contrasted nicely with the bright stainless steel handrails. And I loved the idea that they stood captive for a large swathe of the afternoon, ours and ours alone.

Looking back, I can see that all those buses of years ago helped get me through the drudgery of life as a young schoolboy. Then, they were simply a friendly presence in an otherwise challenging world; now I realise they became much more.

No bus – Newcastle, Gateshead or otherwise – was ever routed along the street I lived on: Northumberland Avenue, a relatively minor residential road linking Ashburton Road with the top of Salters Road. Yet for years I nurtured the fantasy that I would one day see a double-decker drive along it.

My memory tells me I finally did once, perhaps after the driver realised he'd made a wrong turn earlier on the route. The bus in question was one of Gateshead's PD2s. But now that the whole of my childhood bus experience seems somewhat dreamlike, I'm no longer sure if this really happened, or is merely wishful thinking elevated to fact. It would be nice to think it might have.

Happy days in Devon

Peter Shipp

Who went on to buy his own bus company, has happy memories of growing up in

I attended Torquay Boys' Grammar School from 1955 to 1962 and with no car in the family in those days I was a regular customer of Devon General, for whom I would later work as their first 'Traffic Apprentice' when I left the sixth form.

It is rather a long time ago(!) but I recall that with no direct bus from home to school I originally used route 30 from its Babbacombe terminus, a short walk from home, and alighted at Castle Circus, at the top of Torquay's main street, and then walked the mile or so to school – uphill most of the way! My favourite perch was the longitudinal seat for three on the nearside beside the platform where I could talk to the conductor and watch the comings and goings. The buses were almost always DG's 1952 AEC Regent IIIs with stylish Weymann 56-seat double-deck bodies which ran on most local Torquay routes at the time. Occasionally fleet number 679, the Regent with the new 'tin front' and the lone Weymann Aurora body (which never went into production), turned up to provide a

treat as by then my interest in buses had become pretty well established.

After a couple of years I discovered that a better way was to walk the mile or so from home up to St Marychurch and take route 54 which ran right past the Boys' School and on to Shiphay and the Girls' Grammar school – and therein lay the other attraction as several girls caught that bus, unlike the 30 on which I had usually been the only pupil!

Competing for my attention though was the fact that the 54 was often allocated one of the Devon General 'Light Sixes' – buses that had been put together using parts from prewar single-deck AEC Regal chassis and then fitted with Weymann lightweight all-metal double-deck bodies, so quite interesting and, as a batch, I believe unique.

Because the bodies were so light and the buses were only 7ft 6in wide they had a tendency to roll quite spectacularly in the hands of livelier drivers. This route involved a right turn at Castle Circus, at the traffic lights in front of the Town Hall, where there was an

The 'official' school photo of the Upper Sixth Form prefects – Peter made it to deputy head boy. That's him third from the right in the front row.

By Bus to School

A Devon General prewar AEC Regal, rebodied by Weymann in 1953, on route 54, which had the added bonus of girls.
Thomas W. W. Knowles

adverse camber, as the road into which the turn was made continued downhill to the left and into the town centre. Naturally – as youngsters always do – we always sat on the top deck and often on the morning journey there were few if any passengers downstairs.

Thus it was that one day I was seated upstairs on a nearside window seat when the driver saw the lights about to change to red as the bus approached. So he put his foot down and turned right where the camber, the top deck load and the soft springs on the narrow chassis combined to produce a mobile tilt test which must have looked as startling from the outside as it felt inside. I would not be surprised if the offside tyres parted company

with the road but I know that I found myself looking down almost vertically at the road and I think the 30 or so of us upstairs must have felt that our hour had come.

Miraculously we made it and the journey continued as if nothing had happened but I recall that some of the girls used to sit downstairs after that! We boys were made of sterner stuff! Later the route became the preserve of one of the 1952 Reliance/Marshall single decks which were rather less exciting – and rather less interesting anyway.

When I left school and joined DG I had to spend six months travelling on three buses from Babbacombe to Exeter every morning. Happy days!

Just round the corner at the same location – Castle Circus – another Devon General prewar AEC Regal/Weymann rebody on route 30.
Thomas W. W. Knowles

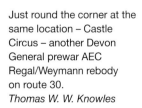

The best part of the day

Brian Souter

Co-founder and chief executive of Stagecoach, recalls 'child neglect' and 'child exploitation'

It was 1959. We had never had it so good and public transport usage was at its all-time high in Scotland. This was the background to my first bus journey from Letham council estate to the Perth Junior Academy, unaccompanied at the tender age of five. What on earth were my parents thinking about? No car trip, no fretting mother at the school door, no risk assessment, no child protection policy – well, no requirement for any of these things. In those good old days people lived in caring communities, children travelled to school with matronly conductresses who kept order, and car traffic wasn't even a factor.

So my mum took me down to the bus stop and, sure enough, bang on time a red Guy Arab utility double-decker appeared out of the mist. Would my dad be driving? Would I be allowed upstairs? What kind of

ticket would I get? How long would I be on the bus? Turned out that this was a school trip squeezed into a country bus working and the tiny old conductress, who smoked roll-ups, seemed to know everyone. Anxious to get all the fares gathered, Cathy had pre-priced some green cardboard single tickets from her 'country punch' and so I happily

The young Brian in 1989 with his father, Iain, a former bus driver with Alexander Midland at Perth.

Brian still goes out on the buses, though not always as literally as at the 2006 Megabus launch.

parted with my 3d and there I was rolling past the smoking chimney pots on my first adventure by bus from our council estate.

I grew to love the school trip and it was the best part of my day. I used to collect the tickets and make my own bus conductor's set, timing myself to see how fast I could collect fares and make imaginary journeys as small children do. In time we got a new bus on our school service – a Bristol Lodekka, which was blue and had no steps downstairs. It was so smooth and fast and didn't roll and creak and whine the way its predecessor did. Our school run ended up on the spare sheet and then we got different drivers and conductors, some of whom I recognised from having their tea break at our house with my father. A lot of my extended family worked on the buses and my cousin, who was a conductor, used to let me travel for free. In fact, one day I gave her 3d and she gave me 6d back – nice deal, but I remember worrying that an inspector would get on and she would be in trouble.

The other memorable bus trip I made as a small child was from Perth to Essendy, near Blairgowrie, on the berry bus operated by A

Brian at the wheel of the former McLennan Leyland Tiger, DGS 625, the berry bus now in Stagecoach ownership.

& C McLennan. These ex-London Transport RTLs were loaded up three to a seat with children heading out to pick raspberries (we now move from child neglect to child exploitation!) At the end of the season they often used single-deck Leyland buses, which were bodied by the company at their Spittalfield workshops. One such vehicle, DGS 625, is still in Stagecoach ownership and I confess I enjoy taking the odd trip down memory lane once or twice a year!

Mischief in Surrey

Ray Stenning

Flamboyant designer and publisher, on growing up in London's Country Area

I was brought up in the green country bus area of London Transport, in that corner of Surrey close to the Kent border, near Oxted. I can remember my Mum taking me to my first day at school, aged five – Limpsfield County Primary – but I can't remember if we went on the bus. I do remember I didn't want to go, but a girl named Gaye smiled at me and then it didn't seem so bad – perhaps I just liked her name.

Mostly I walked to school, but sometimes paid 1/2d (6p) child fare to travel the three stops on a lowbridge RLH on route 410. This was the 1950s and for a while it was still Bell Punch tickets on a rack, hole punched with a ping by the conductor. When I was nine we moved about a mile to a new house at Hurst Green and to get to the same school

I now had to catch a one-person-operated GS on route 464. Actually, in those days it was two GSs in tandem, as they only seated 26. They used Gibson paper roll ticket machines before the RLHs did. To get home, though, me and my schoolmates preferred to walk and spend the bus fare on sweets. If only my Mum knew of some of the mischief we got up to on those walks home … best left unsaid, other than I definitely wasn't a goody-goody!

I passed the eleven-plus exam – three of us did that particular year – and was sent to Purley County Grammar, along with my friend John Keen. This was a bus enthusiast's heaven as it entailed a journey on three different routes with three different types of buses, sometimes more. In the mornings I'd run round the corner at breakneck speed to catch (or just miss) a GS on the 465 to Old Oxted, changing there to a heavily-loaded Reigate-bound RLH on the 410 to Godstone bus garage. You couldn't always get on but some conductors were happy to break the rules and you might be one of 13 crammed in the downstairs gangway. Once it was so busy we had to stand in the upstairs sunken gangway – a 53-seater

carrying damn near 80. Because of the low roof upstairs, and single-skin construction, on a cold, damp day the condensation was horrendous. It would drip on you, but you could stick your ticket to the roof for a bit (it was Gibson tickets by then), peel it off and leave a reverse print on the cream paintwork. You could also turn the upstairs into an amazing wind tunnel by winding down the half-drop windows at the front. Girls with beehive hair-dos loved that – not!

At Godstone John and I had to change again to the then busy, frequent 409 and 411. This was run with RTs and we usually caught the one that had come up from East Grinstead as three schoolmates from Lingfield would be on it – Geoff, Gerrard and Simon. That particular bus would have been based at East Grinstead garage (EG). It was often already quite full, so Godstone (GD) would sometimes send out a Green Line RF (normally used on the 709) as a relief. Sometimes we would get on that and be really lah-di-dah.

In 1962 things changed a bit. As part of London Transport's desire for standardisation, the arrival of RMC-class

Children board London Transport Country Area Routemaster RML2310 outside Limpsfield primary school, photographed in 1966, a year after RMLs were introduced onto the 410.
Ray Stenning

Green Line Routemasters set off a chain reaction. They released some RFs, which in turn replaced some GSs. Our local 464 and 465 (and 485) got RFs from 24 October 1962, only what was rather interesting is that these RFs started out as buses, got converted to Green Lines in the mid-1950s, and here they were back as buses again. They betrayed their bus origins with makeshift parcel racks, not faired-in like those on the purpose-built Green Line RFs. I liked them, because they were a bit special. One was RF313 and it was still in the insipid experimental pale green but with cream window surrounds, until it got repainted. It's interesting that you'd hear people say we had Green Lines on our route now. It wasn't that they understood the provenance of these buses, but RFs were what they were used to seeing on Green Line 707 that dropped into Oxted from London and Croydon once an hour.

London Transport decided the RLHs had to go so that it could make savings by more efficient scheduling of RTs on Godstone's three main routes – 409, 410, 411 – instead of having a separate allocation of lowbridge buses purely for the 410. A game of double-bluff then ensued. London Transport said that if the council didn't lower the road under the low bridge in Oxted it would have to send the 410 with its taller RTs on a rather circuitous route that avoided the low bridge and missed out on the most popular stop by Oxted Station. The council said, go on then, so London Transport did. Public opinion and nasty letters did the rest. By 15 May 1966 the road was lowered and the 410 back on its normal route. But before then something a bit exciting had happened.

The 409/410/411 were the first country routes to get the new green RMLs on 3 October 1965, except they hadn't all arrived in time so we had to put up with red ones for a while, too. I preferred green. I did quite like the slight squeak the plastic window surrounds made and the taut feel to them. Brilliant engineering, well made, good-looking, but was a front-engined, rear open platform bus the best idea for country routes? Probably not. The first one, RML2306, was my favourite, for no particular reason.

In the late 1970s I actually drove school buses, part-time for a couple of companies when I briefly lived in Somerset – Wivey Coaches and Berry's. These were to and from secondary schools along narrow lanes from far-flung rural villages. Most of the kids were fine, but there was one trouble-maker.

London Transport had earlier used RLH type lowbridge AEC Regent III/Weymanns on the 410. This is RLH22 at Reigate. *F. G. Reynolds*

One run I often did was to Kingsmead School in Wiveliscombe. The kid in question had a habit of running up and down, jumping and shouting while the bus was moving. I stopped and refused to continue until he behaved. It worked, only to get his revenge the little blighter told his dad I had been doing well over 70mph. I was summoned to the traffic commissioner's office in Bristol but took along a certificate proving that the Strachans-bodied Bedford

SB wasn't physically capable of more than 39mph. His dad got a snotty rebuke!

That seems a long time ago, and after doing a couple of seasons driving long-distance holiday coaches across Europe to France, Germany, Austria, Italy and Yugoslavia I decided I didn't want to drive a bus or coach ever again. I moved back to London as I had other talents the bus industry was in desperate need of. But it was fun for a while.

The hobby that got out of hand

Mike Sutcliffe MBE

Noted preservationist and Leyland expert, on his High Wycombe schooldays

A young lad's interest in vehicles usually starts with those that he sees every day, and I ran true to type – my junior school was across the other side of High Wycombe, and, even at the tender age of nine, with younger sister Jill age seven in tow, it was sometimes necessary to catch the service bus home. This was operated by the Thames Valley Traction Company (High Wycombe was on the easterly boundary of Thames Valley's operating area), and it would frequently be a Leyland Tiger TS7 or TS8, with Brush or Eastern Coach Works body. On

Mike, age 12, on holiday in Bournemouth in 1955 with his first Woolworth's camera over his shoulder, ready for some serious photography. Behind is a Royal Blue Bristol L6B/Beadle.

that was the place to sit. It was the subject of many arguments. These buses had what looked like a small letterbox in the back panel below the window, and I always wondered what these were – in fact they had been used as a small destination box when new.

I well remember that, during an English lesson at the junior school, a Thames Valley Tiger TS8 with Harrington coach body stopped in the road outside at the Belisha beacon crossing (as they were called in those days). Having not seen one of this batch before, BMO 989 was a real treat. I could restrain myself no longer and said in a loud voice to *all* of my classmates 'Just look

entering the bus at the rear, there was a single seat over the wheelarch on the nearside, and

at that!'. I was instantly reprimanded by what seemed then to be my lifelong enemy 'Old Ma Cabbage', the rather strict headmistress of the junior school, who never

ABOVE: And three years later, Bournemouth 1958, Mike, still in shorts age 15, with notebook and pen in hand and a Hants & Dorset Bristol LWL/ECW coach.

BELOW: Peter Wilks' Comet before conversion to double-deck.

seemed to appreciate the young Sutcliffe's mischievousness.

These old Leylands of Thames Valley were disappearing fast from the fleet, being replaced by ECW- and Windover-bodied Bristols at a very rapid rate, until they had all gone in 1954, although many of them had a second lease of life with showmen. In those days a trip to the fairground was a sight to behold – nearly every vehicle operated had been converted from a bus. One would be treated to sights from a previous generation of motorbuses – many of these I had never seen in service – particularly the Leyland Titan TD1s and Tilling Stevens Express buses, let alone petrol electrics. These ancient vehicles had a special interest to me, though at that stage there was no thought of preservation.

By 1952 we had moved to the outskirts of High Wycombe, on Cressex Road, near Booker aerodrome – this meant even longer journeys home from school on the bus which was invariably Thames Valley no.507, EJB 229, a Bristol K6B with ECW lowbridge body, which became my favourite 'modern' bus of the time.

The local coach operator at Booker was F. H. Crook, a firm that had built up a stage carriage service in the area, which it had sold to Thames Valley in 1937, along with the whole of its fleet of 10 vehicles. With the proceeds a fleet of brand-new coaches was purchased. The most interesting vehicle was not in the modern fleet of runners – it was very much a non-runner, with its nose buried in a hedge next to the garage at Limmer Lane. It was the remains of an REO Speed Wagon registered YK 9541, with a small saloon body built by Wray. Being green in colour it had probably been in this derelict condition since before 1937, and was eminently restorable, but at the age of 11 restoration was restricted to repainting Dinky toy buses into my own

Mike's Pioneer, with electric lighting set, tax-disc holder and rear-view mirror, shortly before its unfortunate end.

recording of these vehicles could take place. However, there was little money to spare and a financial evaluation had to be made before taking each photograph. I well remember on one of my forays by bus into mid-Lancashire, from my Todmorden holiday base. I was at Wigan, having visited the corporation bus garage, and with only two frames left on my film. I was in full school uniform, and a policeman stopped me as he thought I was playing truant, and asked which school I went to. Being totally amazed at the reply 'I come from High Wycombe, sir' he instantly took me to Wigan Pier, and insisted that I took a photograph of this historic monument. What should I do – waste one of my precious frames, or invoke the wrath of the law? I pretended to take a photograph, making the appropriate clicking noise with my mouth, and then pretended to wind on the film. He was obviously convinced and let me go on my way.

These forays into deepest Lancashire became quite a regular thing, and I looked forward to the long school holidays – I would load up my bag with notebooks, pencils, camera and film and, of course, enough currant teacakes to last me for the day and set

fleet livery. It did, however, start my mind thinking! This was not the only wreck in the area because, just around the corner, was an ex-London General S type single-decker, S888. Absolutely complete, it was painted grey and in use as a static caravan – another bus from a bygone age.

A terrible blow struck in 1954 when my father died at the age of 44, when I was only 11. I never therefore had the opportunity to get to know him properly and to share interests with him. From then on virtually everything I did with my hobby was self-initiated. My sister and I were whisked away by my grandparents for a holiday in Lytham St Annes and this was my first introduction to the Leyland 'Gearless' bus – Titans and Lions with the Lysholm-Smith hydraulic torque converters. What a magnificent sound the Titans made with their Leyland 8.6-litre oil engines – there has never quite been an engine noise to match their melodic sound.

In 1955 I was treated to my first camera, a 'VP Twin' which cost the princely sum of 7/6d (37½p) from Woolworths. Now some serious

Mike's restoration activities at age 11 were restricted to repainting Dinky buses into his 'Stirlingshire Traction Co' livery – he thought the name sounded good.

off from Todmorden, catching the bus from town to town. I travelled across Lancashire as far as I could get there and back in a day, visiting all the municipal bus garages, studying buses in their proud municipal liveries – many of them fully lined out and without an advert in sight. Can you imagine a boy of between 11 and 14 being allowed to do that these days, let alone having the inclination to make one's own entertainment?

Already seriously 'bitten by the bug', my first attempt at amateur bus building was around the age of 12 or 13 when I built 'Pioneer'. My school friend, Peter Wilks, from Flackwell Heath, and I visited one another's houses regularly to compare notes on Thames Valley. He, with the help of his grandfather, had converted an old box into a single-decker bus, with the use of some pram wheels and plenty of sacks. The resulting vehicle was named 'Comet' and we had great fun pushing one another about in it along the paths in his large garden. Shortly afterwards Peter added

an open-top upper deck on the contraption and Comet Mark II, from a distance, could almost be confused with a London General B type! However, neither of us dared ride on the upper deck as it was so unstable – it would almost fall over if you just looked at it!

Comet inspired me to build my own bus. Wheels were in short supply as every boy wanted to build his own trolley, but having found some suitable wheels, I first built the chassis. My grandfather found a box that was just right, side pillars were affixed and even a curved plywood roof! I painted it green with a white stripe and a grey roof (the latter being copied from Manchester early postwar livery). It was fitted with a steering wheel and electric lighting, powered by a small battery, with switches and jam-jar tops for reflectors. This was the 'bees-knees' – it could sit two small boys, one behind the other, and needed a lot of pushing with its bus body on. We had an immense amount of fun with Pioneer – either with its body on or in chassis only form.

A Thames Valley Leyland Tiger TS7 at High Wycombe station ready for the journey home on the single seat.
W. J. Haynes

Unfortunately it came to a sticky end – a friend and I were playing with it on the wonderfully smooth tarmac surfaces in front of the Cressex Road shops when five youths hijacked us and made off with Pioneer – two inside it, two pushing and one pulling. They made off with it at an alarming rate, but when turning the first corner and going far too fast, it turned over and the pillars and roof were smashed to firewood. Poor old Pioneer! The only good thing that came out of it was that the ring leader of the louts was one of the two passengers, both of whom were badly shaken and grazed.

In the 1952/3 period there were very few publications aimed at bus enthusiasts. Ian Allan Ltd was the only serious publisher with the quarterly *Buses Illustrated* magazine, and the ABC books covering some of the major fleets. *Buses Illustrated* opened my eyes to the bus industry and every issue was a treat to behold, with 'provincial developments' giving up-to-date details of fleet movements. It also contained advertisements by people such as W. J. Haynes, R. H. G. Simpson, Aviation & Transport photographs, S. N. J. White, Ascough & Taylor, and a host of other people who sold postcard-size bus photographs, and much of my very limited pocket money went in sending off for these. I also discovered a fellow enthusiast, Prince Marshall, who ran a small shop in Vauxhall Bridge Road, London, selling bus magazines and photographs, and I persuaded my mother to take me there on one of her occasional shopping trips to London. It was a disappointment not to find any Thames Valley pictures, but Prince put me in touch with Michael Plunkett (*the* expert on the early fleet of Thames Valley, and of course, the Titan TD1). Both Prince and Michael were to become good friends who gave me support and encouragement in the future.

Many years later this intense interest grew, from the first real bus bought for preservation at the age of 17 to, 49 years later, a fleet of nine immaculately-restored Leylands, which include the largest collection of pre-1925 buses in the world. In achieving this I was proud to be awarded the MBE by the Queen for services to motor heritage in 2004. I suppose really it is just a hobby that has got out of hand! The full story is told in my book '*The Leyland Man*'.

Celtic fringes

Sholto Thomas

Bus company manager, went to school in Swansea and Edinburgh

There's no doubt that my first buses to school instilled an interest in buses and led to my career in the industry. The buses were those most musical of machines, synchromesh-gearbox AEC Regent Vs.

My first primary school at Blackpill, Swansea, only taught the first three years. So at the age of seven I embarked on trips to Craig-y-Nos Preparatory School in Uplands, Swansea, around three miles away on South Wales Transport's service 85. But the buses on the 85 weren't any old Regent Vs. They were the 'Silver Buses' – unpainted Weymann-bodied forward-entrance 529-33 (SWN 992-6). And they had exhaust brakes to add to the aural delights. I was smitten.

A South Wales Transport AEC Regent V/Willowbrook in Swansea in 1963, similar to the buses Sholto caught to school.

Accompanied by another pal and his older brother from our small housing estate, we felt quite superior to our schoolmates who used common-or-garden red SWT buses.

After about a year, we felt confident enough to try other routes, and with a longer walk from the school in the afternoon we could catch the United Welsh 64 Pennard route, the service which ultimately required SWT's last Regent Vs. It got us one stop nearer home and saved an uphill walk at that end. In those days, the 64 had a fine variety of vehicles, many originating with Swan Motors. Some even managed to climb the hill to our destination without a down-change

from third gear to second. I now know that these were preselect 9.6-litre AEC Regent IIIs, compared with other Gardner 6LW-engined fare such as BBW-rebodied Guy Arab IIs, Duple-bodied Arab IIIs, a pair of Bristol KSWs and of course a gradual infiltration of Bristol LDs. Sadly during my first year's infatuation with the Regent Vs, the Swansea & Mumbles Railway had closed, otherwise this too could have featured, subject to the walk at both ends. Indeed whilst waiting for the 85 one morning, we saw one of the trams loaded on the morning Central Wales goods train, its top deck on one wagon, the bottom deck on

One of Sholto's hill-climbing options was South Wales route 80 and the new 'raucous' AEC Renowns, like this 1963 Park Royal-bodied example.

another. How sad it didn't survive at the Middleton Railway whence it was headed that day.

After four years it was time to move on to Dynevor Grammar School, located right in the middle of Swansea town centre. This change also coincided with a family relocation to the Swansea Valley end of town. I was provided with a season ticket for the five-mile trip to school, valid on South Wales Transport, United Welsh and James of Ammanford services, and although the latter had been absorbed by SWT the previous year, its fine livery was still to be seen. All combined to provide roughly a bus every ten minutes into town, but my regulars were the SWT 18 from Brynamman in the morning which fielded tin-front lowbridge Regent III/Weymann Orion no.1174 (JWN 901) and in the afternoon SWT service 1 for Ystradgynlais, usually one of a batch of Regent V/Willowbrook 572-7 (12-17 BWN),

based at Pontardawe depot. If I missed the 1, the next bus was the United Welsh 18, which further up the valley confusingly had a different destination to the SWT 18, and could be any of Clydach depot's Bristol FS, FSF or FLFs with either Bristol BVW or Gardner 6LW engines. There was a relief bus for a while (though the United Welsh crews seemed quite happy to pack in passengers well over the authorised capacity), this being a Bristol LS or MW, though once an ex-Thames Valley LL6B, complete with cobwebs (I kid you not) turned up, and proceeded to astonish me with its lively performance. The morning SWT stalwart, no.1174, was in due course replaced by a 36ft AEC Reliance 590/Marshall, whose wonderful gearbox music was tempered by alarming body movement for a brand-new vehicle. The ex-James service 121 usually served up 36ft Leyland Leopard/Marshall 950-2 (893-5 DCY), ordered by James but delivered to

Edinburgh Corporation three-door Leyland Leopard/Alexander, no.101, on the 45 route with clear instructions where to board. *Gavin Booth*

Sholto's alternative route home from school in Edinburgh was to use service 1 either way in a huge semi-circle round the city. Standard fare was the 1966 batch of unusual Pneumocyclic Leyland PD3/Alexander and there were sharp hill-climbs to add interest. *Gavin Booth*

SWT, backed up by an occasional Tiger Cub. Another difference compared with travel from the Swansea Bay side of town was that many bus crews and passengers conversed in Welsh.

During this time Ian Allan launched the first edition of *British Bus Fleets 18 – South Wales*. Not only did it give us details of all these vehicles, but also the ones that we never saw in Swansea. I say 'us' because bus spotting became quite a rage at Dynevor (most of us were rail enthusiasts too). Some of us would occasionally catch a bouncy Bridgemaster over to Swansea East Dock loco shed in our lunchtime to see what was there, or latterly what had arrived to be scrapped locally.

Our school games field was, somewhat bizarrely, located on the top of Swansea's Townhill. No special transport was laid on so we had to make our way up and down by SWT buses on the famous routes involving the 1 in 6 hill. At that time these services were allocated a fleet of Monocontrol AEC Reliances and since no standing was allowed on the hill, our year of around 150 pupils somewhat swamped things.

Another hill-climbing option on my way home, if I had a few spare coppers, was to catch service 80 via Clase to Morriston and then my usual route the rest of the way.

Clase, also now the site of the DVLA, is a housing estate at the top of one of Swansea's many hills. The 80 at that time had new AEC Renowns, far more raucous than the Regents, and which had to drop down to bottom gear on one of the more severe grades. Stirring stuff.

In 1966 we moved to Edinburgh. Our family home was situated in an area quaintly known as Holy Corner – it had a church on each corner of the local crossroads. There was a bus stop right at our door, served by Edinburgh Corporation's 45 service, direct to my school which was George Heriot's, just a mile or so from the centre of the city. The 45 in those days was operated by a fleet of Pneumocyclic Leyland Tiger Cubs, dreadful underpowered things with appalling vibration if anything near high revs were used. Few drivers could time the gear changes well either, so neck-snapping progress was also part and parcel of the experience. Wonderful. The famous three-door Leyland Leopard/Alexander Y type no.101 (YSG 101) was a regular too, but I can only once remember the conductor in its seated position. We still had to enter 101 at the rear, to the consternation of many who failed to appreciate the frontal variation between a

Weymann body and the unique Y type, or notice the sign on the front of 101. In the morning a duplicate bus was scheduled, for a while a 5LW-engined Guy Arab II/Nudd rebody, though one week we were treated to a Duple Bella Vega-bodied Bedford SB.

Our games field was, again, a few miles from school, Eastern Scottish being contracted to take us there. Bristol Lodekkas were the standard fare but occasionally an AEC Bridgemaster or the Renown would appear. In those days Edinburgh Corporation Transport had a flat fare for schoolchildren, so my return to home at the end of games did not have to

be by the direct service 23, run with some of the 300 extremely-boring Orion-bodied Leyland PD2s. My alternative was to use service 1 either way in a huge semi-circle round the city and walk the last 10 minutes home. The batch of unusual Pneumocyclic Leyland PD3/Alexander 826-50 (EWS 826-50D) performed on the 1 and there were a few sharp hill-climbs to add interest.

So there you are. What a selection of vehicles! How could I fail to be an enthusiast? Which led a few years later to driving and managing buses to school.

Those lazy hazy crazy days of summer

David Thrower

Bus preservationist and author, makes musical connections

Why is it that memories of one's childhood are so pin-sharp, almost half a century later, yet we struggle to remember what one was doing only yesterday? No doubt a psychologist, or amnesiologist (if there is such a profession), could give us some clues. But those bus rides

to school from those early years, say from age seven to age 16, are still firmly lodged in the brain, and are as crystal clear as though they were … well, yesterday …

As a schoolboy, I was lucky in the bus-riding-experience sense, in that I moved around more than many of my

David now has his own RT, 2794, here at the Worcester Park running day in 2008.
David Thrower

Northern General's forward entrance Routemasters were favourites of David. *T. W. Moore*

contemporaries and was able to sample three very different and varied operations, in three very contrasting parts of the UK. Gavin Booth, in his book *British Buses In Colour*, headed each chapter with the title of a contemporary pop record and I am going to shamelessly plagiarise his idea with a very slight variation, by titling each of my own three school bus rides (actually, there were five, but all will be explained) with the names of musicians of the time.

The Nat King Cole era

When I think of Nat King Cole, I immediately think of Sutton, Surrey, not because the late great singer hailed from there (which of course he didn't) but simply because his gentle voice was in the charts at the time I went to school in what was and still is very genteel and pleasant suburban South London. Home was at the north end of the town, school was at the south end, and the distance was perhaps the better part of two miles (interplanetary, for a seven year old). In those now far-off days of the comfortable 1950s, those lazy hazy crazy days of summer 1958 and 1959, Sutton was a truly wonderful place to be for anyone interested in buses, with red RTs working the north-south direction along Sutton High Street, green RTs working east-west on the 408/470, and Green Line RFs on

the 711 and 725, these two intersecting at the town's crossroads at the Cock Hotel (long demolished), plus short B1 trolleybuses on the 654 from Sutton Green (my nearest stop) to Crystal Palace.

What was my strongest memory of travelling on my routes, the 164/164A/80/80A? Of never having to wait very long for a smart RT to arrive. Of one of my bus-interested classmates running for a bus and missing his footing, then being dragged along on his knees as the conductor frantically rang about 20 emergency bells for the bus to stop (I can still see it now). Of a kindly conductor getting off his bus and crossing me over the Brighton Road on my very first day. Of the 1958 strike, and walking to and from school for week after week. Of seeing my very first Routemaster, CRL4 (which became RMC4) on trial on the 711 (the bus queue stared at it, stunned, in awe). Of a fare of just a penny-halfpenny (half a penny, in decimal money). And of an amazing, standardised, smart bus fleet that I now know was probably the greatest in the whole world, ever.

Enter the Shadows

All this was to abruptly change for me when we moved to Derry (no one ever called it Londonderry) in 1959. Bus route to school?

There wasn't even a bus route to anywhere! We had to walk a mile along a winding lane, frequented by speeding Royal Navy Landrovers and Bedford SB buses, to a place called Enagh Lough (yes, it really was a lake, as the name implies) and catch a bus run by some lofty organisation called the Ulster Transport Authority, to then travel five miles into Derry and then catch another bus that looked vaguely like a London Transport TD across Derry City. To say that this was a culture shock is an understatement and I look back and wonder that I was trusted to undertake this, at barely age nine, with some considerable amazement. Where did the Shadows come in? Well, via the charts, of course, though by the time 'Apache' was Number One our collective mothers had organised the UTA to provide a proper service all the way from our new housing estate at Strathfoyle, Derry's answer to a New Town, to Derry City, with an onward extension to our Victorian-mansion prep school, where the bus would later wait for us outside the gates, like a faithful dog, at 3.15pm.

And what were my memories of those years? Of the bus's schoolchildren noisily arguing who was going to win the November 1960 US Presidential Election (to my everlasting shame, as a politically illiterate ten year old, I backed Nixon). Of insert-Setright ticket machines, and of using rubber bands to fire folded-up tickets the length of the bus, the missiles zinging past (or occasionally into) ordinary passengers' ears. Of being profoundly impressed with what I think were Albion Aberdonians with UTA-assembled turquoise-coloured Metal Sections bodies to Alexander styling, displacing some of the dark green and cream 'TDs' (actually, Leyland PS1s or PS2s with UTA bodies). Later, we moved to the edge of Derry, and sampled further PS1s and PS2s, many (or even all?) of which had roof-racks and, utterly amazing to London eyes, a ladder up the back, like the Deadwood Stage. Wells Fargo! The Wild West! The latter image was reinforced by the town's bus station in The Strand, a low ranch-type building with a wooden boardwalk where one expected John Wayne to tie up his horse at any moment, swagger into the bus station cafe and shout 'OK, Kincaid, go for your gun'. About as far from those trolleys turning at Sutton Green as you could get, short of emigrating to Timbuktu.

The last day of trolleybus operation in Newcastle, 1 October 1966, with a London-style BUT 9641T/Metro-Cammell at Denton Square.

One of Northern General's 36ft AEC Reliances with Willowbrook bodies.

The Animals versus The Byrds

My final school bus rides (actually, my truly last journeys to school were back in London, on the tube, but that's well outside our piece) were from Chester-le-Street to Newcastle upon Tyne and then in later teenage years from Heworth (today of Tyne & Wear Metro fame, but in those days people used to reply 'Where?'), to Worswick Street bus station and on to Jesmond, travelling onwards by, whilst they lasted, those great gliding yellow leviathans, the Newcastle trolleybuses. The Chester-le-Street route was jointly Northern General and United Auto, so it was a straight fight between an allegiance to Bristol FLFs (in the morning) and either Guy Arabs or Routemasters in the afternoon (no prizes for guessing where my affections lay). Later, by the mid-1960s, on the Sunderland Road routes, I was to enjoy a galaxy of Northern or Sunderland District PD2s, PD3s, Tiger Cubs, Northern Reliances, Sunderland District BET-style 36ft Leopard single-deckers, Routemasters and (as they say in adverts) 'much, much more'. This was variety to bewildering levels. I could even use Newcastle Regent IIIs and Vs and Gateshead PD2s, PD3s and Atlanteans, if I wished.

Then it was onward across Newcastle by those beautiful trolleybuses. The Animals topped the charts with 'House of the Rising Sun', but the sun set on the trolleys within a couple of years, to my great sorrow, leaving unused wiring and gaunt poles in silent reproach as the Byrds sang their West Coast (of America) rock. The most intense memories of those times, in terms of buses, were the Routemasters arriving brand-new, where they made a great impact, and of Newcastle's smart Alexander Atlanteans displacing the trolleybuses as well as the AEC Regents and PD2s of the Corporation fleet. The Atlanteans in particular created a very dynamic and futuristic impression and still rate in my mind as a memorably excellent piece of styling. Other very vivid memories were the wonderful sights and sounds of Worswick Street, of the trolleybuses whining northwards along Northumberland Street (in my mind I can still see the wires vibrating and hear them strumming, as I sat in the front upper deck seat), and the unbelievable galaxy of public transport vehicles one could witness day after day on the Tyne Bridge, at Marlborough Crescent bus station, or the Haymarket. Happy days indeed, and how I wish we could recreate them, even if only for a moment.

So what do you do?

George Watson

Transport consultant, recalls a stand-off in his days as managing director of Clydeside Scottish

Faced with one of the most intensive deregulation bus battles in the country, Clydeside Scottish, like many other state-owned bus companies, faced a real dilemma; what to do with bus services provided for non-statutory travel to and from schools.

The problem was simple. Resources (buses) were financed and maintained solely for the carriage of schoolchildren making short trips under the statutory limit (two or three miles). The very length of these journeys implied very low fares, typically 8p or 10p in those days.

In the cross-over period from regulation to deregulation managers faced a number of dilemmas including criticism for abandoning schools services. So in some ways we were hoisted by our own petard when in some places we continued to offer the services, perhaps justified by winning baths contracts between the peaks.

But in other cases peak resources were fully committed to this work and as improved performance was the mantra (not least to

answer critics of the Glasgow bus wars), it was clear that doing nothing was not an option.

And Strathclyde PTE, unlike many of their colleagues south of the border, resisted introducing a child concessionary travel scheme.

So we in Clydeside Scottish decided to remove the general half fare concession in the morning peak. This was aimed at either encouraging SPTE to introduce the concession (with follow-on arguments about the viability of dedicated services) or maybe encouraging parents to find alternative transport – but this carried big risks in a competitive scene.

Come the day there was resistance from parents, despite giving them advance notice, and drivers found it difficult to implement the increase.

So we received notification that a petition was coming in to us, and in due course a BBC camera crew arrived followed by the police with a protest group of around 40 people. I duly met the protesters led by (SPTE) Councillor John Mullin and attended by the police. I was

During his time at Clydeside Scottish, George famously introduced former London Routemasters on the busy services around Glasgow and Paisley. This, RM652, was the first. *Maxwell H. Fowler*

presented with a 6,000-name petition (100 single-deck bus loads?) and accusations of being 'not on' (a powerful argument) and 'blackmailing the parents'. The BBC televised a full report of the demonstration and interviews with both John Mullin and myself.

John Mullin made the usual arguments – too long a walk for five-year old children, the parents who were unemployed couldn't afford the increase, safety of children, etc. I pointed out the problem of vehicles standing through the day, and the associated costs that were estimated to be four times more than the revenue (at least!). In fact the BBC's conclusion was very balanced, after 30 minutes the demonstrators left unsure of what to do next.

Later, following advice from on high, we reverted back to an all-day child fare structure but the prevailing discounts for children were reduced. Over time the number of scholars services was reduced but the problem never completely went away in my time. We had no more encounters with the protesters - but it was an interesting moment!

Variety in Sunderland

David Wayman

Writer and photographer, on the sights and sounds of the buses of his Wearside youth

My 2.1-mile two bus ride to Sunderland's Bede Grammar School for Boys from September 1952 until July 1957 formed three sides of a rectangle. Lunch time at home meant eight bus rides daily. All vehicles were operating on normally scheduled service journeys (unless otherwise indicated below).

My first bus of the day, on a five-minute frequency service, had commenced its journey a mile to the west. After heading easterly for 0.6 of a mile on a purely local road it turned left to meander four miles to its terminus, staying south of the River Wear. I sprinted 50 yards the other way, to the stop for my second bus. Usually its journey had commenced at

The curving front of 1938 Sunderland Corporation Roe centre entrance-bodied Daimler COG5 no.53 contrasts with the squarish lines of the Massey wartime utility body on no.66, a 1943 Guy Arab II. *R. Marshall*

A luscious Sunderland line-up with, nearest the camera, the writer's favourite, no.58, the 1942 'unfrozen' all-Leyland Titan TD7. Beyond are ex-Stockton TD7/Roe no.25, ex-Blackburn 5LW Guy Arab II/Pickering utility no.5, and 'native' Guy/Massey and Daimler CWA6/Duple utilities.
D. S. Burnicle

the seafront, three miles north-easterly across the river. It was now heading southerly on its 10-minute frequency service for 1.2 miles along the B1405 ring road, then would climb westerly on the A690 for 0.4 of a mile to the school gates before continuing a further mile. The half-fare initially was a penny (1d) on each vehicle, increasing later to three-ha'pence (1½d). During 1952/early 1953 the conveyance on either or both morning journeys would usually be one of the following buses. A 1946 8.6-litre Daimler CWD6/Masseys (four in fleet); a 1946/47 8.6-litre Crossley DD42/3 /Cravens (three) or Crossley Manchester-style body (six); a 1947 AEC 9.6-litre Regent III/Roe (six); a 1949 8.6-litre Crossley DD42/7C /Crossley Liverpool-style (six); a 1948-51 8.4-litre Daimler CVG6/Massey (12) or Roe (22); or a 1952 8.4-litre Guy Arab III/Roe (12), 11 with preselectors and one a melodious constant-mesh box. The Crossleys had constant-mesh gearboxes except for the 1949 and all had Gardner 5LW engines from 1950. All Daimlers and AECs had preselector gearboxes. All were 56-seaters except the 1952 Guy Arab III/Roes, which were 58-seaters.

Unladen weights had reached eight tons but now were to drop to about seven. In mid-1953, eight so-lightened 58-seat Roe-bodied Daimler CVG5s arrived, followed in early 1954, partly for tram replacement, by 20 and later 12 more of that combination and two batches of 12 Crossley-bodied preselector 5LW Guy Arabs, plus five CVG5s with locally-built and most rare Associated Coachbuilders bodies. The last Daimler/Roe delivered had 65 seats and all others, 58, although the future standard was to become 63. All double-deckers from 1954 had 'new-look' frontal features.

Sometimes, however, my second bus would be an 'extra' that had commenced its day on expeditions to the docks, shipyards, marine engineering works or factories and therefore likely to be one of the following types. There were 1934-39 Daimler COG5/Roes (30 of them), 1942 Leyland Titan TD7/Leylands (four), a 1943 Guy Arab I/Roe, 1943 Guy Arab I/Pickerings (two), 1943 Daimler CWG5/Masseys (two), 1943/44 Guy Arab II/Masseys (13), 1944 Guy Arab II/Pickerings (two), 1944 Guy Arab II/Masseys (two), or 1944 Daimler CWA6/Duples (three). The COG5s, three of the TD7s and the 1943 Roe-bodied Guy had 48-seat centre entrance bodies.

Plenty of variety, then!

The entertainment from a Daimler COG5 included much sweet and resonant singing from the five-speed preselective gearbox. 'First speed' was a most rarely-used crawler. Performance was quite adequate for the work to be done. In its day, the Daimler

Associated Coachbuilders of Sunderland produced only five double-deck bodies. Sunderland 1954 Daimler CVG5 no.169 here represents this batch while the conductor holds it steady.

COG5 probably offered the best combination of economy and reliability with advanced specification. In the lively wartime CWA6 the dominant sound was that of the thumping AEC 7.7-litre engine. Gardner 5LW-engined Guys performed ponderously but 'got there'.

Upon boarding a centre-entrance bus, when passengers reached the third step they could without a further step either turn left into the forward part of the lower saloon, right into the rearward part, or continue ahead to the upper saloon. The staircase was Y-shaped with a double-width stem of two steps leading to two single-width five-step prongs that curved through 180 degrees. From December 1952, the livery changed from red-and-cream to green-and-cream for all but centre-entrance buses.

It was the sight of a Leyland Titan TD7 approaching, however, that induced joyful jumps. The Leyland-bodied one had been diverted from an order placed by Western SMT of Kilmarnock and was finished to its specification, including black stanchions. I would certainly vote the TD7 the most entertaining type of bus ever. Starting from rest, usually in second gear, it would emit a sobbing-like transmission sound, accompanied by a convulsing forward movement as the drive was taken up. The more vigorous the start, the better the entertainment. That refined, flexibly-mounted Leyland 8.6-litre oil engine with subdued, distinctive intake roar, transmitted practically no vibration to the body. Moreover, due to the heavier flywheel,

Who else rode Atkis to school? Sunderland's two Roe-bodied L644LWs had Roe bodywork with a single doorway of dual width as illustrated here by no.31. *C. W. Routh*

upward gear-changes took longer as the revs died away more slowly. There was a humming-top sound from the flywheel, rising and falling on the musical scale with engine revs through each gear ratio. Sheer bliss!

At mid-day, in both directions of the home trip my third to sixth buses were usually from the same selection as the day's first. Come five minutes past four, however, outside school my seventh was usually a delicious Daimler COG5, the eighth bus also likely to be from the same selection as the first. From 1955, however, optionally I used a new half-hourly trans-suburban service connecting home and school, with single-deck one-man-operated buses. This widened the vehicle scope to include two Roe-bodied 35-seat 5LW Guy Arab IIIs (forward-engined) of 1950 and four 42-seat dual-door Burlingham-bodied 5HLW Guy Arab 5HLW LUFs (underfloor-engined) of 1954, designed for driver-only operation. All six had preselectors and on the Arab IIIs part of the front bulkhead had been removed in order to create a gap wide enough for fare transactions to take place alongside the driver's left shoulder. In 1956 these six Guys were joined by a full-fronted 41-seat Roe-bodied Atkinson 644LW EXL, a lorry-derived chassis with 5.6-litre Gardner 4LW forward engine. The Atki, to be joined by a similar one in late 1957, had acoustic effects somewhat similar to those of the Bristol L5G with characteristic Gardner 'bark'.

I blame the Luftwaffe

John Whittle

Retired transport executive, on childhood days in Tooting and Glasgow

Our esteemed editor has suggested that, for many, school journeys by bus first awoke an interest in buses. My interest in transport and buses in particular started much earlier, however, when I was a toddler living in Tooting, South London during the late 1930s.

Shopping trips with mum to the market at Tooting Broadway were a special pleasure. Not only did I get a delicious red toffee apple from one of the stalls but I could feast my eyes on the transport delights on offer, trams, buses, trolleybuses, underground stations and Green Line coaches, the whole spectrum of the LT operations. I could have stood all day gazing on these wonders.

Then I started school, which was but a short walk away. Most walked to school in those days but I still enjoyed the trips to the market on Saturdays.

But Adolf Hitler disrupted this and September 1939 saw me evacuated to Chichester. There, Saturday matinees at the Odeon were followed by many happy hours opposite the Cathedral watching the magnificent Southdown buses reversing into a side street with the conductor guiding the driver by loud whistle blasts.

Dad had served in World War 1 (he lied about his age and joined up at 16). Now over the call-up age, he worked at the army supply depot in Deptford. The Luftwaffe couldn't resist such a target so it was moved to Rouken Glen to the south of Glasgow, dad going with it. It was decided the family should be together in Scotland as a temporary measure until the war ended. There is nothing more permanent than the temporary and we never did move back to London.

My first school in Glasgow was again but a short walk. That changed when I moved up to Shawlands Senior Secondary. This meant a journey by corporation bus, usually on one of Larkfield garage's Daimler CWA6s. These were pleasant vehicles to travel in and I enjoyed the combination of sounds from the AEC engine and the Daimler preselector. I boasted that I travelled to school on a Daimler but few friends were deceived into thinking the Whittle family must be very rich! Later, we moved further out, to Thornliebank. As it was beyond the Corporation's monopoly area, I used Western SMT's. Neilston-Glasgow service for my school journeys.

One of my schoolmates, Gus, had an uncle who drove for Western on the Newton Mearns route, including a journey passing the school just after 4pm. We often took a trip with him to Newton Mearns and back, in the front seat where we could watch him of course. His regular bus was a Leyland Titan TD5 and we enjoyed many a spirited run to the terminus where he would allow us to inspect the cab and change the destination. Bliss! Later he changed to a shift on the Neilston service which included the journey we took home after

school. Like most drivers, he took intense pride in his bus and carried dusters and polish to keep the cab clean. He was furious after a day off at finding the relief driver had been smoking and had littered the cab floor with ash!

On first acquaintance, the Neilston service was operated by handsome Leyland-bodied TD4s and TD5s. Towards the end of the war the SMT group converted a number of single-decks, mainly Tigers, to double-decks and fitted new semi-utility bodies by Alexander. The bodies had a considerable resemblance to the Leyland designs and, to me, were among the most attractive of the wartime buses. A batch was allocated to the Neilston service and became my regular conveyance. In the struggle to catch up on the arrears of maintenance from the war Newton Mearns depot had to resort to borrowing buses from other depots and subsidiary companies to maintain services. I can remember travelling on two such buses, both Leyland Titans – an elderly TD1 from the Rothesay Tramways fleet and a lowbridge TD4 in the yellow and red livery of Dunlop, Greenock. Exciting times!

After the war, new buses began to appear. In 1948 Newton Mearns depot received several Leyland PD1s with Leyland's own bodies and some were allocated to our Neilston service. My first sight of one

One of the all-Leyland Titan PD1s allocated to Newton Means depot – 'the height of modernity' in 1948 – that left John gobsmacked.

approaching the stop at the school left me gob-smacked. The deep windscreen and wide chrome radiator seemed the height of modernity. I can still remember the aroma of leather and paintwork in a brand-new bus. I remember too the gentle hum of the heater motor, such luxury! When Gus's uncle allowed a peek in the cab, the instrument panel with its snazzy square dials impressed me greatly.

When I started a career in transport, I embarked on four year's study for the examinations of the Institute of Transport. This meant four nights a week at the College of Commerce in Glasgow, giving me another travel-to-school experience. When classes finished at 9pm I would proceed to the bus stop at Charing Cross, accompanied by Mr Takahari, a very knowledgeable man who lectured on several subjects. One night I asked him to expand on some point he had made in the economics class. He launched into a detailed explanation during which he crouched down and drew diagrams with his finger on the pavement. The bus queue suddenly became a very enthralled audience!

During my time at Central SMT, I experienced the school bus from the supply side. Local authorities had a duty to supply transport for pupils travelling over a certain distance, Mainly, they discharged this by purchasing season tickets for the children to travel on the regular services. We also carried many children who lived closer to the school and didn't qualify for free travel. In addition to considerable duplication at school times, several special services operated where the ordinary services didn't penetrate, sometimes, in response to requests to save younger children crossing busy roads. This meant our resources were fully stretched at school times. We did achieve some alleviation by persuading a few schools to stagger their starting and/or finishing times but such co-operation was not easily secured.

Unruly behaviour isn't a new phenomenon and we had our share but our conductresses were generally more than capable of maintaining order. I suspect several youngsters' behaviour improved after a 'clip round the ear' from one of these denizens! Vandalism was also beginning to be a problem. When a bus returned from a school run with its seats slashed, there was little sympathy from the school. The headmaster obviously considered it our problem, not his. Frustrated, I advised we weren't prepared to tolerate this and the service would be withdrawn. Uproar ensued. Parents protested that their 'little darlings' had to walk, local and national politicians jumped on the bandwagon and the Traffic Commissioner insisted that we restore the service. The most annoying element was that none of those making a fuss attributed any fault to the children.

On moving to Scottish Transport Group's ferry operation, I encountered a different dimension of the school journey. Many of the islands we served were too small to support a secondary school and too distant for daily commuting. A number of pupils travelled to Oban, staying in lodgings all week and returning home at weekends. Special early Monday morning sailings from Mull and Lismore catered for them.

A similar situation applied to the Island of Cumbrae on the Clyde. Although very close to the mainland, it was then in the County of Bute so the children travelled to Rothesay. On Mondays, a special early ferry took them to Largs whence they were taken by bus to join another ferry to Rothesay, reversing the process at the weekend. This took them past a perfectly good school in Largs which would have allowed them to return home daily. But this was in another authority's area and it seemed beyond the wit of the two councils to co-operate to improve the lot of these children!

A north-west London schoolboy

Tony Wilson

Bus photographer and part-time conductor, as a spotty youth in Edgware in the 1950s and 1960s

Without wishing to sound Monty Pythonesque but things were different when I was a lad... Indeed, when I was a wee lad, the lure of the bus came about when I visited relations in Wiltshire and Dorset. For a lad born and bred in north-west London it must seem somewhat of a heresy to admit that one's favourite bus is not something big and red from either the AEC or Leyland stables but something hailing from Bristol in the west and Lowestoft in the east. With parents who hailed from the West Country it was the sights and sounds of Bristol Ks, Ls and LSs that stirred me and in my imagination I was guiding one of these handsome creatures along the Weymouth Esplanade or through the city streets of Salisbury. But circumstances intervened and my young thoughts of the 1950s to be at the helm of such vehicles came to nought.

Borderline was the result of my 11-plus back in 1958. Then a spotty youth, I cannot remember much about it now, as I was not particularly concerned about such things. But I assume it meant a lot more to my parents as they apparently agonised for ages about whether to send me to the secondary modern where my older brother went, or to the local grammar school. In the end they opted for the latter.

Was this the right decision? One will never know. That said, the result could well have been the catalyst that set me on the path, or indeed the platform, to a healthy interest in public transport. For it was to Orange Hill Grammar School in Burnt Oak, north-west London that I was sent. To get there from my home on the Broadfields Estate in Edgware meant quite a trek (well it was then for this spotty youth), down on to the Edgware Way to wait for a big red London Transport diesel-engined umpty-um horse-powered double-decker omnibus on the 107, 113 or 142 bus route. These red beasts would then trundle me down into Edgware Station where I transferred on to a single-decker on the 240A, which in turn would transport me up Hale Lane to the

A London Transport RT on the 113 at Edgware Station where Tony transferred onto a 240A.

Tony almost felt some stirrings of regret when the TD type Leyland Tiger PS1/Mann Egertons like this one at Edgware Station were replaced by the AEC RF-type. *Gavin Booth*

Green Man at Mill Hill and onto a 52, another big red double-decker, and thence to the school down Deans Lane.

Initially I knew very little about these AECs and Leylands other than they would turn up and take me to school in the morning and bring me home in the evening. But the more I travelled on them the more I took interest in their external shapes and their internal design, not forgetting their 'voices', those graunches and grunts as they trundled on their way. Don't worry – I shan't delve too deeply into the minutiae of cogs and throttles and horse-power and suchlike; these things have really been anathema to me. I am more of a 'like-the-look-of' man, leaving the mechanics to those who know about that sort of thing. However, I did get to the stage where I could identify the differing sounds that emanated from a Regent a Titan or a Tiger. But a common feature of these vehicles was that they had a crew. Up front was a driver and on the back a conductor and, as a lad, this struck me as another possibility for future employment, though it never really came to fruition. I say 'really' because more recently I have had the opportunity to fulfil that particular talent. However, that is for another story on another day.

Back to the buses that transported me to and from school. The 52 route was firmly in the grip of the Leyland RTL class and the 107, 113 and 142 routes in the hands of the AEC

Regent RT type, whilst best of all, the 240A, was operated by a small allocation of TD-class Leyland single-deckers. These were really in the winter of their lives but to me had more than enough guts left in them to climb the hills along the route. I believe I almost felt some stirrings of regret when a few years later they were withdrawn from their sterling service and replaced by the AEC RF-type.

Which led me to wonder where these vehicles had come from – the 107 from over the hills at Borehamwood and particularly the 113 from Oxford Circus. Of course with this one my imagination ran wild and I tried to get my parents to take me there so that I could see

Tony's Ian Allan London Transport ABCs from his younger days with the TD type Leylands faithfully underlined.

By Bus to School

Tony used London Transport RTs on the 142 – here in Kilburn High Road – to reach the 240A at Edgware Station.

the circus animals and clowns. Little did I know then that it was in central London. Then there was the 142 from somewhere called Watford and the 52 took you all the way to a place called Victoria. As for the 240A, this was the best as it was like a switchback ride, with some of the hills that were climbed along the route. But those sturdy little TDs took them all in their stride. As time passed, my interest in these monarchs of the road grew, with their bodies from Mann Egerton, Park Royal, Weymann and the like and, on closer inspection, I noticed there were numbers on the sides. Around about this time I was introduced to the publications from Ian Allan and soon was marking down my observations. I met some like-minded individuals at school and we gathered together to swap thoughts and observations and gradually I found out more and more about this wonderful world of the bus.

Then there was the advent of the London Red and Green Rovers that opened up even more and soon helped me to discover, like a Drake or a Columbus, new worlds over the horizon. Exotic places such as Aldgate, Camberwell,

Now Tony can be found as a part-time conductor for Cumbria Classic Coaches.

Kingston and Staines in the red area were visited at one time or another, all the time returning home with the spoils to transfer the scribbled numbers into underlinings in the relevant ABCs. And then even more adventurous were the journeyings into the green areas around London where the likes of Dunstable, Grays, Dorking and Windsor would all be graced by a visit, not that anyone took notice of me in any of these locations.

Then it was my brother's turn. He introduced me to the delights of capturing some of these buses on film. It was a trusty Box Brownie that was the first of a succession of cameras to be pointed buswards. A small collection of black-and-white prints then began to appear in my bedroom. Some while later he handed down yet another camera, but on this occasion it was to make a much greater impact, setting me on the path to 40-odd years of colour slide photography. Today, digital imagery has overtaken all this, but I will always have a certain fondness for the late 1950s and early 1960s, which still provide me with some wonderful memories of my developing years.